Interior Landscape

DESIGN MEDIA PUBLISHING LIMITED

© 2014 by Design Media Publishing Limited
This edition published in April 2014

Design Media Publishing Limited
20/F Manulife Tower
169 Electric Rd, North Point
Hong Kong
Tel: 00852-28672587
Fax: 00852-25050411
E-mail: suisusie@gmail.com
www.designmediahk.com

Editing: Tong Jialin
Proofreading: Catherine Chang
Design/Layout: Cao Lin

ISBN 978-988-12969-7-9

Printed in China

Interior
Landscape

DESIGN MEDIA PUBLISHING LIMITED

PREFACE

From the Garden of Eden, the gardens are manmade paradise on the earth; extraordinary examples among them are the terrace gardens in the Apennine peninsula by the Italian cardinals, the Islamic courtyards in Granada by the Moor, the Suzhou gardens by the Chinese merchants. One model is the Lion Court of the Alhambra Palace in Spain, in which cruciform canal symbolising "water""milk""wine""honey", extend from the courtyard into the hallway, bringing coolness in the hot summer. It is a best combination of function, form and meaning.

However, the gardeners had not enough knowledge or technology to plant healthily indoor gardens until in late 20th century, the new science and technology make it realistic. The modernism took a big step forward in architecture and garden design, John Portman in Atlanta Grand Hyatt designed an atrium up to 22-storey with tall trees bathing in sunlight. By the early 2000s, the French botanist Patrick Blanc invented "vertical garden", which growing plants on the wall become possible. Thanks to his innovation, interior landscape developed from the horizontal to three-dimensional.

On the other hand, along with the development of urbanisation, more and more human beings live in urban area. The statistics show, the urban population spend 70% to 80% of their time in the indoor space, especially the infants, the elderly and disabled persons even longer; indoor air pollutions cause shocking harm to the respiratory and cardiovascular. The indoor gardens could lower the temperature, increase humidity, absorb harmful gases, etc. The plants are irreplaceable in these functions. The other function of a green space with plants is the gardens can relieve nervous tension.

We are looking for more green space in the urban area, and an indoor garden is no doubt a good beginning for a healthier city. This book has presented some of the world's latest cases, to show the readers the interior landscape of new design concepts and design techniques. Architects, landscape designers, related engineering and management staff can take this book as a good reference.

CONTENTS

Chapter One

Interior Landscape:
Creating a Green Microclimate

1.1 Why Choose Interior Landscape?

Interior landscaping has become increasingly popular during the last 30 years. Most architects now include plants in their design specifications for new shopping centres, office complexes and other public areas, and they are something we all expect to see when we walk through the door (Fig.1.1). But what is it about plants that make them such an important building accessory?

Fig.1.1 ASTER AADHAR HOSPITAL, designed by ar. Shirish Beri. The well ventilated, sky lit arrival atrium with plants, reception counters, waiting and circulation lobbies.

The most obvious answer is that they look attractive – who can fail to be charmed by the graceful arch of palm leaves or the exotic beauty of orchids? However, recent research has shown that the value of plants goes far beyond the purely aesthetic. Plants are actually good for the building and its occupants in a number of subtle ways and are an important element in providing a pleasant, tranquil environment where people can work or relax.

The key uses and benefits of plants are summarised below.

1.1.1 They help to reduce sickness absence.

Absence from work cost British business £11.8 billion in 2002. Job dissatisfaction and low morale can be prominent factors in short-term absence and could account for as much as 15% of all reported sickness absence. Employers can tackle this most easily by re-examining people management policies and the working environment, to see what can be done to improve staff productivity and well being. If companies with the worst absence rates could meet average levels, the UK economy would be £1.9 billion better off.

1.1.2 They improve the indoor environment.

There is now general agreement within the scientific community that plants improve the indoor environment, and are useful weapons in the fight against the modern phenomenon known as sick building syndrome (SBS). No specific cause of SBS has been identified, but poor air quality, excessive background noise and inadequate temperature and light control are thought to be important factors. Because plants have a large surface area and exchange water and gases with their surroundings, they have a unique ability to tackle many environmental problems. In particular, plants can:

• Reduce levels of carbon dioxide, which can accumulate in buildings from the breathing of its occupants and the by-products of heating systems and electrical equipment.
• Increase relative humidity, which should be between 40% and 60% RH for maximum human comfort.
• Reduce levels of certain pollutant gases, such as formaldehyde, ben-

zene and nitrogen dioxide.
• Reduce airborne dust levels.
• Reduce air temperatures.
• Reduce background noise levels.

1.1.3 They can be used to soften/hide less attractive features.

However well designed, most buildings have features that are best kept covered, such as service areas, storage facilities and harsh structural elements. Plants, with their wide range of size, shape, habit and leaf form provide an elegant solution that is both attractive and functional. Fig.1.2 and 1.3

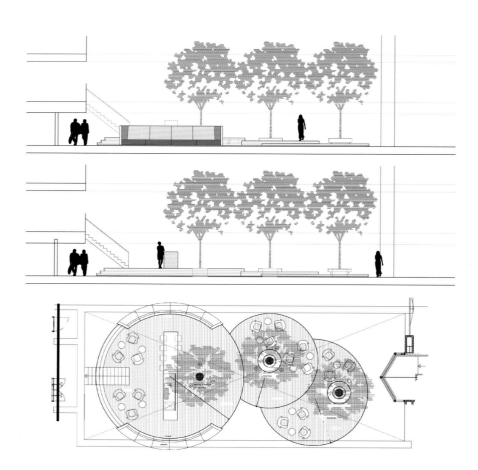

Fig.1.2 and 1.3 Ploum Lodder Princen Law, designed by C4ID
interieurarchitecten.

By creating a new link between the main entrance of the building and this entresol, it became easy to make a new routing for both the employees and the clients. In that way the base of the void became the new meeting place for everyone. Surrounding that with meeting rooms and completing it with a high-end coffee bar made its success almost obvious.

1.1.4 They can be used to break up large open areas.

The vast expanses of open space found in airports, stations, shopping malls and open plan offices look soul-less and intimidating unless "broken up" by familiar objects. Plants are the most common solution, providing natural divides and reference points that make the space look more friendly and inviting.

1.2 Green Buildings: the Role of Interior Plants

The Green Building movement is gaining strength in many countries. Developers, especially governments and local authorities, often set the trend by commissioning buildings built to recognised "green building" standards.

The main motivation in building to such standards is that "green buildings" are much more energy efficient than conventional buildings and, consequently, cost less to run. However, there are other factors that motivate developers to adopt "green building" standards, including a desire to enhance their image as responsible corporate citizens or employers, or to increase the lettable income from the buildings.

Interior plant displays can contribute to a good green building rating in many ways, not all of which are immediately obvious.

1.2.1 What are "green buildings"?

"Green buildings" are buildings that have been built or refurbished to a set of auditable standards that reduce the negative impact of the building on the environment. Initially seen as a "nice to have" feature, developers are increasingly specifying that buildings should be as environmentally friendly as possible.

1.2.2 Where do interior plant displays fit in?

The above are all very worthy and make good sense, but how does interior landscaping fit in and contribute to the "greening" of a building (apart from the literal effect caused by presence of foliage)? In all the cases listed below, plants have a useful role to play.

1.2.3 Use of grey water and rain water

Grey water is that which has been used once, for instance to wash hands or dishes, and then recycled for re-use where drinking quality is not required, e.g. toilet flushing. Grey water is usually treated in some way to remove particles and is often sent through a reed bed where biological processes help with the degradation of materials such as detergents. Once treated, the water is reused for applications that do not require potability. Grey water is, in most cases, suitable for watering both indoor and outdoor plant displays.

Rain water is a free resource that is seldom exploited. Many commercial buildings have large roofs and other surfaces that would be ideal for capturing rain water. This water could be used in the same way as grey water and would be ideal, if not beneficial, to interior and exterior plant displays.

1.2.4 Cooling

One of the benefits claimed for interior plants is that they help cool the air around them through evapotranspiration. The effect is genuine, but limited as in most cases, rates of evapotranspiration in offices are low due to limited light and humidity. However, atrium planting can certainly help with temperature regulation in some buildings. Fig.1.4 and 1.5

Plants reduce the solar power received by the building, thus regulating the surface temperature of the structure against the sun. They help retain humidity and weaken the "heat island" effect. A supporting steel structure protects the south and west facades from sun radiation. The greenery stops sun rays from getting through in the summer seasons, while in winter the lack of leaves gives access to more lighting indoor.

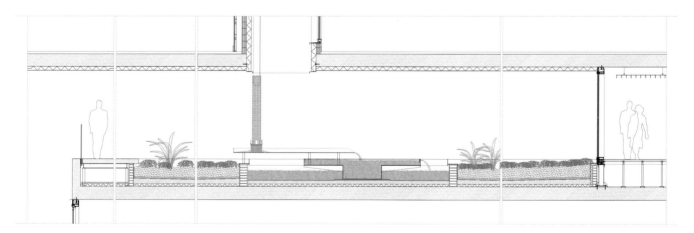

Fig.1.4 and 1.5 The water accumulated in the water reserves located under the ground floor generates around itself a space of vegetation which contributes to the temperature regulation of exterior zones during the summer. 100% of the water accumulated is treated and reused both for the irrigation system and for the use and treatment of sanitary waters. It is also used in the structure's cooling system by evaporation.

1.3 Concept of Interior Landscape Design

Great indoor garden lies in the eyes of its creator. So, while the principles of interior landscape design are great guidelines to follow, don't feel like they're the "have to rules" of landscaping. Abstract and creativity are allowed.

1.3.1 Unity

Unity should be one of main goals in design. It may be better understood and applied as consistency and repetition. Repetition creates unity by repeating alike elements like plants, plant groups, or decor throughout the landscape. Consistency creates unity in the sense that some or all of the different elements of the landscape fit together to create a whole. Unity can be achieved by the consistency of character of elements in the design. By character, it means the height, size, texture, colour schemes, etc. of different elements. The principle applies to all other elements such as groups of plants and materials. A simple way to create unity in the landscape is by creating themes. Fig.1.6

1.3.2 Texture

Texture can be defined as the relationship between the foliage and twig size, and the mass of the plants. Close up, texture comes from the size and shape of the leaves, the size of twigs, spacing of leaves and twigs, the colors and shading, the gloss or dullness of leaves. etc. At a distance, texture comes from the entire mass effect of plants and the qualities of light and shadows.

1.3.3 Simplicity

Simplicity is actually one of the principles in design and art. It's one of the best guidelines you can follow as a beginner or do it yourselfer. Just keep things simple to begin with. Simplicity in planting, for instance, would be to pick two or three colors and repeat them throughout the garden or landscape. Keeping decor to a minimum and within a specific theme as well as keeping hardscapes such as boulders consistent is also practicing simplicity.

Fig.1.6 Gran Terraza Lomas Verdes, designed by Grupo Arquitech. It features a set of tall vertical planting, fountains, pavilions and seating area, consistent in height, size, textures and plant species.

1.3.4 Balance

Balance in design is just as the word implies. There are basically two types of balance in landscape design. Symmetrical and Asymmetrical. Symmetrical balance is where there are more or less equally spaced matching elements of the garden design. With a garden equally divided, both sides could share the same shape, form, plant height, plant groupings, colors, bed shapes, theme, etc. Asymmetrical balance on the other hand is one of the principles of landscape design that's a little more complex. While textures, forms, colors, etc. may remain constant to create some unity, shapes and hardscapes may be more random. This form of balance often has separate or different themes with each having an equal but different type of attraction.

1.3.5 Natural transition

Natural transition can be applied to avoid radical or abrupt changes in your interior landscape design. Transition is basically gradual change. It can best be illustrated in terms of plant height or color but can also be applied to all elements in the interior landscape including but not limited to textures, foliage shape or size, and the size and shape of different elements. In other words transition can be achieved by the gradual, ascending or descending, arrangement of different elements with varying textures, forms, colours, or sizes.

1.3.6 Proportion

Proportion simply refers to the size of elements in relation to each other. Of all the principles of interior landscape design, this one is quite obvious but still requires a little thought and planning. Most of the elements in interior landscape design can be intentionally planned to meet the proper proportions.

Chapter Two

Design Elements of Interior Landscape

2.1 Nature and Architecture: the Interior Design of Hard Landscape

Fig.2.1 and 2.2 Interior of shopping centre "Ceramic City", designed by Artline. The interior landscape of the lounge area consists of a range of fountains, mosaic tiles and decorative lighting of different texture as well as plants.

Hard landscape means any area devoted to a landscape made up of hard wearing materials such as stone, concrete and other construction materials, as opposed to soft landscaping which is grass, bark and other such items. Fig.2.1 and 2.2

It is better to have a preference for natural materials (or look-alikes) as well. Floor coverings, even if not made of wood, stone or slate are made to look as if they were. In offices, shopping centres and even hospitals, where utility and economy are of great importance, it is possible to use natural products (or recreate the look and feel of them) through the art of interior landscaping. Many products are available, and they don' t have to look twee or old-fashioned: cutting edge design is possible.

There are many dozens of plant containers available that are made from natural materials. Wood, woven banana leaves and palm fronds, bamboo, cork, sea-shells and mother-of-pearl are all used and come in every shape and size imaginable.

By using materials such as gravel, shingle or slate quarried from the vicinity, it is possible to create a local feel to an interior landscape.

Hard landscape are increasingly aware of the demand for sustainable materials and the impact of the carbon footprint and "green" credentials on today's society and remain committed to demonstrating sound environmental performance of their activities, products and services.

2.2 Base Coverings (Paving)

Base covering or in other words paving is the material which covers the ground as the finishing layer to give a good walking surface. Base coverings define the space and general layout of the landscape design. The material should be chosen with care, taking into consideration colour, texture and functions. They should be sympathetic to their surroundings, blending with the mood of the space and the materials of the other design elements in the space. Using many different materials, especially in a small space is not a good idea. It will confuse the eye and create a restless effect in a space (Buczacki, 1999).

The base covering materials which are used in interior volumes are different than those used for outdoor spaces. Since the subject of this study focuses on interior spaces, the ones which are preferred for interior spaces will be explained in more detail. The common materials mostly being used in interior spaces are: carpet, area rugs, laminate, ceramic tile, stone (granite), wood and other floorings.

2.2.1 Carpet

Carpet is a floor covering woven or felted from natural or man-made fibers. Fitted carpet is attached to the floor structure, extends wall-to-wall, and cannot be moved from place to place . Area rugs are another type of carpets. The difference is that they can be moved from place to place and usually come with a bigger variety of color and texture. Therefore, they are used as decorative elements for flooring. Carpet brings the sense of comfort to the interior volumes. Therefore, they are used for covering of the children play ground, restaurants, shopping malls, hotels, offices or homes, completely or partially. Carpet stay bright and clean if maintain properly. However, they are not advised for public spaces like shopping malls, restaurants etc because, it is too difficult to keep hygiene in public spaces.

2.2.2 Laminate

Laminate is a kind of floor covering that appears similar to hardwood but is made with a plywood or medium density fiberboard ("MDF") core with a plastic laminate top layer. Laminate may be more durable than hardwood, but the finishing is different from hardwood. Laminate flooring may have different patterns which can resemble different woods coverings or ceramic tile. It usually locks or taps together. This material can be installed easily and cleaning is easy since it has a very slight (glossy) surface. It is suitable for interior spaces but normally it's used in private areas more than public interior volumes like shopping malls or offices. Because it needs special care since it can scratch even with the moving of furniture on the surface.

2.2.3 Wood flooring

Different species of wood are fabricated into wood flooring such as Plank and Parquet flooring which is a type of hardwood flooring and known to be durable and more environmental friendly type of hardwood flooring. They might have different texture and color. Wood is a material which needs special care. It can't be used without considering the climatic conditions; moist of the area, sunlight (if it gets to the room), heat of the space and etc. What differs wood flooring from wood laminated flooring is that laminate acts as a plastic cover but pure wood flooring is usually used on places which gets less moisture and is less crowded areas such as houses or office spaces. They can partially be used in shopping malls.

2.2.4 Stone

"Natural stone is a dramatic and unique way to accent any environment. The natural beauty of stone creates an elegant and warm setting"(http://www.expressflooring.com/stone.php). Different natural stones are cut into a variety of sizes, shapes, and thicknesses to be used as flooring. Stone flooring is usually set in mortar and grouted similar to ceramic tile. Furthermore sometimes, cracked stones are used in a rock pool in an interior volume for decoration.

2.3 Secrets of Interior Waterscape

Water is essential to survival, but it also tends to take it for granted. However, when human beings lived in a more natural environment, being close to a reliable source of water really was a matter of life. Whilst there are complications associated with plumbing into a water supply and the ongoing maintenance of water features, there are many benefits to be gained by their presence in a building. If there is a built-in water feature, in an atrium for instance, or even a tank of tropical fish, plant displays can be used to draw attention to it. In some locations, there may be a view over a water feature, pond or lake in the grounds of the building – these features can be incorporated into the interior landscape design by using them as a focal point and drawing an observer's gaze beyond the boundaries set by windows. However, where it is impractical to install water features there are alternative ways to bring water into a building.

Studies showed that art aided recovery, and nature scenes were the most effective. Scenes of lakes, water falls, rivers and the sea will be most welcome in the sterile environs of many modern buildings and can even be incorporated into murals or video art installations projected onto walls.

The sound of running water, babbling streams or even waves breaking on a beach can be recreated with sound-effect recordings and even the smell of freshly-fallen rain or the salty, ozone-like smells of the seaside can also be brought into an interior landscape by selecting an appropriate fragrance for use in ambient scenting systems (although such fragrances should only be used in areas of transient occupancy, such as atriums and social areas, rather than in continually-occupied spaces such as offices). Fig.2.3

Fig.2.3 Interior of shopping center "Ceramic City", designed by Artline, Recreation Area at the 2nd floor, Decorative fountain

Landscaping elements such as water elements or plant materials have the potential to reduce average indoor temperatures to below the outdoor average. Landscape can be used to make buildings perform well in hot climates, but may be even more valuable in improving the performance of existing buildings, since most landscape elements can be added without changes to the building itself.

Water is a highly varied design element and may take on such various forms as flat, quiet pools, falling water, and jets of water. Water can be used in the landscape as a purely aesthetic element or it may be employed for such practical functions as cooling the air, buffering sound, irrigating the soil, or providing a means of recreation. The key to understand the water of architecture is to understand the architecture of water; what physical laws governs its behaviour, how the liquid acts and reacts with people's senses, and, most of all, how it effect human beings.

Water possesses several physical properties such as plasticity, motion, sound and reflectivity. These properties influence the purpose and method by which it can be used in interior landscape.

Water has various functions such as climate control, recreation, sound, aesthetic and psychological. According to which functions water is to fulfill in an interior space, the landscape architect should decide what type and character of water meets these desired functions and apply them on the design.

Some of the more common visual functions of water based on its type of motion and character are:

I) Active water elements: Flowing water, falling water, jets and combination water features are examples of active water elements. As it is understood by the name these functions are used where motion or sound is required. The flow of water can be slow and relaxing, or swift and exciting, depending on the nature of the setting and the preferences of the landscape designer.

II) Passive water elements: Sometimes no movement of water is needed. Reflectivity and air cleansing are the functions where passive water elements are used.

2.3.1 Indoor ponds and waterfalls

There is something soothing about having an indoor pond especially if there's the sound of running water with it from a waterfall, or perhaps even just an indoor waterfall on its own. Adding lighting effects to an indoor pond or waterfall, will transform it at night into a spectacular feature too. Fig.2.4

Fig.2.4 The Dubai Mall, Internal Waterfeatures, by ICN Design (Simon Morrison, Richard Jones) AquaWorks (S. W Hooi). In one of the towering domes, a huge waterwall with rippling white water cascades down to the darkened pool some four storeys below.

In confined spaces

If it is limited for indoor space then one of the variously sized natural or sculptured and glazed boulders with a small shallow waterfall from its center can be very effective. Alternatively small multi-level troughs with waterfalls tumble down them, in a variety of designs and materials. Fig.2.5

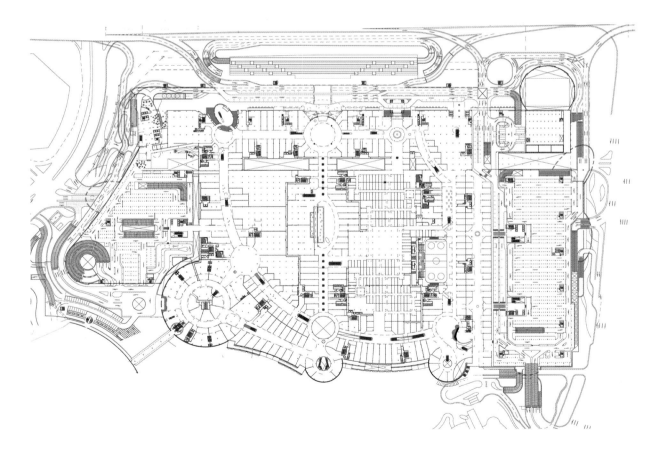

Fig.2.5 The Dubai Mall, Internal Waterfeatures by ICN Design (Simon Morrison, Richard Jones) and AquaWorks (S. W Hooi). It is a series of water features crafted to fit within the building's internal spaces and that would be appropriate to the activity of that particular zone within the mall. The twelve original water features ranged from cascading waterwalls to subtle channels, reflective pools to graceful fountains, all designed to contribute to the experience of visitors, guests, diners and shoppers. Each souk (styled internal marketplace) has a focal space, an atrium or roof terrace, an arcade or plaza for which an appropriate water feature was developed to add to the atmosphere.

Particularly effective at an entrance is to have a sculptured human or animal form, often based on classical mythology, that incorporates either a waterfall or possibly a shallow fountain. Within a limited space a pond could be so small as to make it lose the effect, unless the indoor pond that covers at least 6 square feet.

Larger indoor ponds

Whilst an Indoor pond can be sunk into the floor of a building it is more usual to build the pond on top of a floor. Any suitable pond building material can be used so, such as fiberglass pond, construct a brick or wooden frame into a pond liner, or if the floor is strong enough make a concrete pond indoors. Fig.2.6

Fig.2.6 The Dubai Mall, Internal Waterfeatures, by ICN Design (Simon Morrison, Richard Jones), AquaWorks (S. W Hooi). In the Gold Souk there is a symmetrically patterned pool in the tradition of the paradise garden court.

Stocking an indoor pond with fish is a possibility, but it must have a pump to aerate the water and be careful that the water temperature doesn't vary too much, according to the ambient room temperature. Buy plants for an indoor pond that will be quite happy not receiving direct sunlight and, if the pond will be seen by many people during the evening, install LED lights around the side of the pond, and even under the water itself.

Larger indoor waterfalls

An indoor waterfall should be heard as well as seen and there are two ways of achieving this – either by the height the water falls from or the depth of the trough that it falls into. To avoid a noisy indoor waterfall, but still want to have a tall indoor waterfall, then the noise can be reduced by having a soft lining in the trough with lots of plants or stones, or a series of ledges and bumps for the water to fall down – acting like a water baffle.

During daylight seeing the ways that light catches on the waterfall can be quite mesmerizing and keep that effect going at night by illuminating waterfall; using waterfall LED lights that periodically change colours can be particularly effective.

Electrical safety

Any indoor water feature with an aerator or a waterfall effect will need a pump to drive the water, whilst solar/light powered pumps are available, depending on the location of water feature. The same also needs to be considered if there are electric lights for the indoor pond or waterfall – water and electricity don't mix well together.

2.3.2 Tips for indoor water gardens

An indoor water garden adds serenity and makes an aesthetic statement to interior. Continually incorporate design and maintenance practices to add drama, interest value and years of enjoyment.

Containers

Enamel pots with matching trays work well to allow entry and exit points for hoses. A concrete birdbath can be repurposed into an attractive indoor water garden.

Statuary

Statues are exceptional choices to give an indoor water garden a thematic
design. Fig.2.7 and 2.8

Fig.2.7 and 2.8 The Dubai Mall, Internal Waterfeatures, by ICN Design (Simon Morrison, Richard Jones) and AquaWorks (S. W Hooi). The human sculptures in the huge waterfall are made of waterproof metal alloy, adding dynamic characteristics to the indoor water feature.

Placement and lighting

Choose an interior location that will make the water garden dramatic. Consider a wall-mounted feature at the end of a long hallway with overhead track lighting or a water garden placed in the foyer to greet guests.

Cleaning

Algae growth is the biggest foe of an indoor water garden. Clean the "pool" container, rocks and accent features with a calcium elimination product every month.

2.4 Working with Nature: Lighting and Ventilation

The uniform lighting found in so many buildings may be efficient, but it frequently lacks character and is often harsh. The elimination of shadows and the lack of movement reinforce the sterile, artificial character of many buildings. Poor lighting quality is also frequently cited as a contributor to sick building syndrome. Dappled shade and gentle movement of shadows played through the foliage of interior plants can provide interest and enrichment to the indoor environment.

Combining decorative lighting with plants (or by placing plants in a way that they interact with the lighting already in place) can produce some interesting effects and break up the sterile monotony of many large, open-plan spaces. Plants with small leaves or delicate fronds can be placed near windows to provide dappled shade without blocking out too much useful daylight. They also have the additional benefit of helping to keep warm buildings cool in summer.

Decorative lighting, such as low-voltage LED lights placed among the foliage of plants, could be considered as part of an interior landscape design. They can create the illusion of daylight showing through the vegetation and cast interesting shadows. LEDs are naturally cool, so the risk of heat damage is lessened and they can be powered by batteries or even solar cells. White LEDs are also a potentially useful source of supplementary lighting for plants in darker areas or green walls. Fig.2.9

Fig.2.9 Refurbishment of Zanderska huset, Karolinska Institutet, designed by Inga Varg. The large roof-lights provide high amount of daylight to the entrance hall but is also the result of sustainable intentions. Within the main entrance, a tall free-standing wall rises with growing vegetation on one side and an artwork representing hanging leaves by Ulla Forsell on the other.

2.4.1 Functional lighting: lights to keep plants alive

The conditions inside buildings are very different from those in nature so interior landscapers need to understand how different plants use light and how they adapt to life indoors.

Light spectrum

Photosynthesis may take place only in the presence of chlorophyll, a magnesium containing pigment found in the leaves and stems of all green plants. Chlorophyll absorbs light most strongly in the red and violet/blue portions of the spectrum and least strongly in the green portion. Hence, when natural light shines on a plant mainly green light is reflected and the specimen appears green.

Light sources

The light that indoor plants receive comes from many different sources. Both daylight and light from artificial sources are used by the plant for photosynthesis. Natural daylight, if available in sufficient intensity and duration, is the cheapest and best. However, the amount of sunlight getting through to the inside of a building can be surprisingly low. Outside on a bright, sunny day there may be 50,000 lux (1 lux = 0.093 foot candles), but the absorbing or blocking effects of glass, blinds, furniture, walls and the shading from surrounding buildings can reduce this to a few hundred lux inside a room.

For interior landscapes, artificial light often needs to be provided as a substitute or supplement for natural light. From a plant's point of view, the quality of the artificial light depends on the type of lamp providing it. There are three main types of artificial lights used in buildings, incandescent, fluorescent and gas discharge. They are described below.

Halogen lighting

Halogen lights are a type of incandescent lamp that are increasingly popular in buildings. They are small but produce a lot of light and they are often mounted as spot lights. The quality of light produced is satisfactory for plant growth, and there are some very nice "plant lights" sold as an accessory for indoor plant displays. There are, however, two disadvantages that must be considered.

First, many halogen spotlights are focused on a small area, so if they are to be used for plants, it is essential that correct light measurements are made. Illumination levels drop off rapidly away from the centre of illumination.

Secondly, the bulbs get very hot. They should not be placed too close to the leaves of a plant, otherwise the they will be scorched. A distance of at least 50 cm is recommended.

Fluorescent lighting

Fluorescent lighting is probably the most common in offices, restaurants and other commercial buildings. Most are designed for a maximum output in the 550nm band (green/yellow) and are therefore not ideally suited to plant growth, as the 440 nm and 660 nm bands are deficient. However, some specialist fluorescent tubes reproduce a much fuller spectrum and are becoming more popular in offices where they have been shown to benefit people as well as plants. Compact fluorescent luminaires that replace standard incandescent light bulbs are becoming increasingly popular as they are economical to use and relatively inexpensive to buy. Some compact fluorescent luminaires are also available with near daylight quality.

High pressure discharge lighting

High pressure discharge lamps based on mercury were, until recently, widely used in horticulture. However, mercury has now been largely displaced by metal halide and sodium. Both have a high radiant efficiency and are probably the best types of lamp to use where high light levels are required. Metal halide lights give the best spectrum for photosynthesis and, as the light appears white, are often suitable for buildings where appearance is important. This type of lighting is unusual in offices, but can be used in atriums and other large spaces in buildings such as factory floors.

Plant light requirements

Whatever the light source, a plant's first "instinct" when installed in a building is to orientate its leaves towards the strongest light source. This is most easily observed near a bright window, where the leaves will turn rapidly to face the sun. However an interior plant's long-term chances of survival depend on its ability to adapt to low light levels. It may do this in several ways.

By rearranging the light-trapping chloroplasts, they are all on the upper surface of the leaf. This ensures that they are facing the light rather than being randomly distributed throughout the leaf.

By losing leaf variegation, e.g. in species such as Hedera helix, Epipremnum aureum and Ficus benjamina. The increased amount of chlorophyll in the previously unpigmented parts of the leaf helps to trap more light. By stretching new growth towards the light. The spindly stems and small leaves of Ficus benjamina under low light are a good example of this.

By dropping leaves, so that a smaller "area" of plant is competing for the available light. To get the best out of a plant it is therefore important to know the light levels available and to choose species accordingly.

The light requirements of individual species have been determined after several years of research and experience. It is surprising to think that most of the plants used in interior landscapes evolved in tropical or subtropical environments where light levels are often very high. The Yucca, for example, originally comes from the arid and semi-desert regions of America where light levels are extremely high, yet it can survive in offices where the light is only 1000 lux.

Detailed light requirements of plants can be found by using the plant selector or a to z plant search utility.

Note: Plant light requirements vary around the World due to the different conditions under which the plants were grown and acclimatised by nurserymen. In Europe, plants are acclimatised to much lower light levels than in North America, so what would be considered high light in the UK may be thought of as rather low in the USA. However, the relative light requirements of interior landscape plants seem to be the same. For example, a species such as Dracaena deremensis "Janet Craig", which is a "low light" plant can thrive under 200 lux in the UK but would need 750 lux (75 fc) in the USA. Likewise, a 'high light' plant such as a Yucca elephantipes might need 1000 lux in the UK but in the USA 1500-3000 lux(150-300 fc) is recommended. The Dracaena would be classified as "low light" in both countries and the Yucca as "high light" in both countries.

Effects of buildings

The light that reaches a plant in a building is made up of a lot of complex interacting components. The total illumination reaching individual plants in a building is the sum of the artificial illumination inside the building (e.g. ceiling lights) and the daylight that reaches the plant from outside.

Different types of building will have different lighting characteristics. Large, open shopping centres, leisure centres or atria may rely on daylight as a major source of illumination. Offices and restaurants may have relatively small windows and solid ceilings, and direct illumination by sunlight may be limited to only an hour or so a day. It should also be remembered that Natural light may fall by more than 50% for every metre that you move away from a window.

Atriums and high glass buildings

Buildings with glass roofs or where large expanses of glass make up the walls on more than one side will experience several hours of direct sunlight. In these cases, the amount of artificial lighting may appear insignificant, or may not exist at all during the summer months. The tracking of the sun across the sky will ensure that at some point in time, almost every part of the building interior will experience direct illumination, although for most of the time, high levels of indirect illumination will occur. Fig.2.10 and 2.11

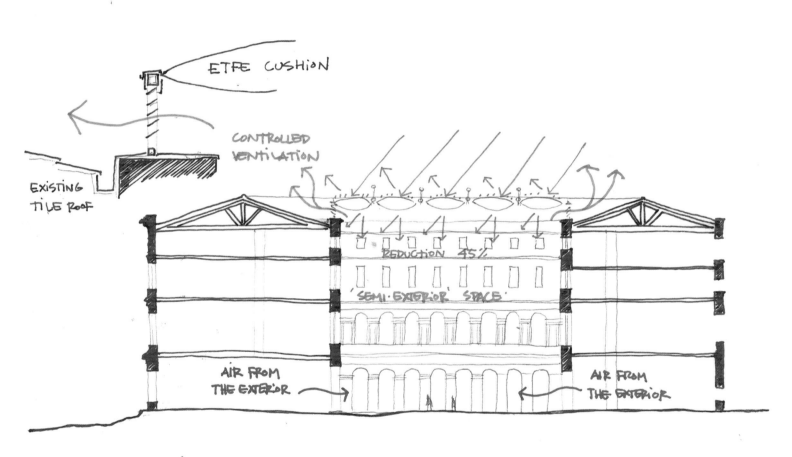

ETFE CUSHION

CONTROLLED
VENTILATION

EXISTING
TILE ROOF

REDUCTION 45%

'SEMI·EXTERIOR' SPACE

AIR FROM
THE EXTERIOR

AIR FROM
THE EXTERIOR

CLOISTERS. THERMAL IMPROVEMENTS.

Fig.2.10 and 2.11 Refurbishment of Deusto University, designed by ACXT. The illumination through the glass roof of the atrium brings sufficient energy to the interior plants.

Offices and buildings with smaller areas of window

Locations where there are only small areas of window will not experience much direct illumination from the sun; any direct illumination will be for a very short time. North facing windows will experience no direct sunlight except for a few hours at either end of the day during mid-summer. Most daylight illumination will be indirect.

Illumination

The brightness of light as experienced by the eye (illumination) is measured in lux (foot candles in the USA, 1 lux = 0.093 foot candles). This is the form of light measurement that most interior landscapers and architects use.

When measuring the light levels in a building for plants, the following points should always be considered.

Natural light may fall by more than 50% for every metre that you move away from the window. Levels should be measured exactly where the plant is to be installed and not simply in the general area. This should also be borne in mind before moving a plant to a new position.

The contribution made by artificial lighting should be assessed, for example by taking readings with the lights both on and off. In many situations this is the predominant source of light.

Allowance must be made for the time of year at which readings are taken. If the light level on a bright summer's day is just enough to support a particular species it will probably struggle to survive in the winter months.

With large plants, light levels in both the upper canopy and lower branches should be taken into account.

Dust and grime on the surface of leaves can greatly reduce their ability to absorb light. Regular cleaning is therefore very important, especially in low light levels.

Once light levels have been assessed, plants can be selected according to their known light requirements and by the application of sound judgement. Fig.2.12

Plants are organic and like people they can have differing strengths and weaknesses. In a single batch of plants there may be several resilient individuals able to cope and acclimatise, together with less dynamic plants that are easily stressed and which may never recover. A strong plant will often have the ability to adapt and cope with either higher or lower light levels than its classification.

Plants react to several different factors, i.e. light, heat and water. These factors interact with one another causing a plant to respond differently if any one single factor is changed. As temperature differs, so does a plant's suitability to a particular light regime.

2.4.2 Ventilation
Ventilation in architecture
With an increased awareness of the cost and environmental impacts of energy use, natural ventilation has become an increasingly attractive method for reducing energy use and cost and for providing acceptable indoor environmental quality and maintaining a healthy, comfortable, and productive indoor climate rather than the more prevailing approach of using mechanical ventilation. In favorable climates and buildings types, natural ventilation can be used as an alternative to air-conditioning plants, saving 10%-30% of total energy consumption.

Natural ventilation systems rely on pressure differences to move fresh air through buildings. Pressure differences can be caused by wind or the buoyancy effect created by temperature differences or differences in humidity. In either case, the amount of ventilation will depend critically on the size and placement of openings in the building. It is useful to think of a natural ventilation system as a circuit, with equal consideration given to supply and exhaust. Openings between rooms such as transom windows, louvers, grills, or open plans are techniques to complete the airflow circuit through a building. Code requirements regarding smoke and fire transfer present challenges to the designer of a natural ventilation system.

Fig.2.12 The atrium is provided with sufficient natural light. A large interior garden is also built here.

Natural ventilation, unlike fan-forced ventilation, uses the natural forces of wind and buoyancy to deliver fresh air into buildings. Fresh air is required in buildings to alleviate odors, to provide oxygen for respiration, and to increase thermal comfort.

Types of Natural Ventilation Effects
Wind can blow air through openings in the wall on the windward side of the building, and suck air out of openings on the leeward side and the roof. Temperature differences between warm air inside and cool air outside can cause the air in the room to rise and exit at the ceiling or ridge, and enter via lower openings in the wall. Similarly, buoyancy caused by differences in humidity can allow a pressurised column of dense, evaporatively cooled air to supply a space, and lighter, warmer, humid air to exhaust near the top. Fig.2.13

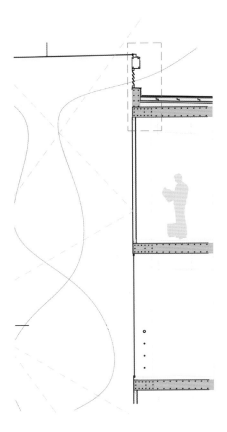

Fig.2.13 The controlled ventilation and artificial illumination provide suitable environment of the growth of the interior plants.

Natural ventilation used by the plants

Suitable ventilation and lighting help enhance the photosynthesis of the plants as it is a crucial process for their nutrient accumulation and abundant nutrition is beneficial for plant growth. Ventilation helps in the respiration of plant roots and facilitates the absorption of minerals.

Ventilation is essential as the air exchange helps protect plants against pests as well.

Plants consume carbon dioxide in the process of photosynthesis, during which carbon dioxide reaches the pores via diffusion. The level of carbon dioxide near the pores decreases as it is absorbed by the plants, which will affect further absorption. Ventilation can bring the density of carbon dioxide near plant leaves to the normal level, thus accelerate the whole absorption process. Fig.2.14

2.5 Living landscape: interior plant design

2.5.1 Plant Materials

Plant materials present a touch of life and beauty in an environment. The landscape designer's expertise with regard to plant material lies in a systematic knowledge of its functions and a sensitive, skilled ability to utilise it in the context of a given design. This includes an understanding of its design characteristics such as size, form, colour, and texture and knowledge of its growth habits and necessities.

It should be understood by the landscape designer that plants have a psychological effect upon people. It calms and relaxes people with their appearances and/or smell. Visual plant characteristics include features related with plant size, form, colour, foliage type, plant texture. These characteristics greatly affect the design process in interior volumes. Therefore, detail information will be given about these issues in the following sections. Fig.2.15

Plant Size

Size is one of the most visually significant characteristics of plant material and it should be studied at the beginning of plants selection for a design.

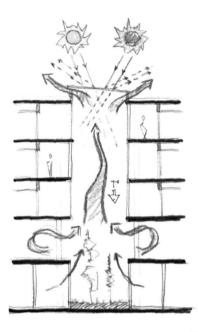

Fig.2.14 Controlled ventilation enhances the exchange of air inside buildings, providing beneficial living environment for the plants and improving the air quality as well.
Fig.2.15 Gardens by the Bay, designed by Grant Associates, Wilkinson Eyre Architects. Horticultural Themed Gardens, designed by Grant Associates with planting by NParks. these gardens showcase the best of tropical horticulture and garden artistry. Together with mass flowering and coloured foliage landscape, they form a spectacle of colour and texture and fragrance within the Gardens, providing a mesmerising experience for visitors.

Plant size directly affects the scale of a space, compositional interest, and the overall structure of a design. Scale is also an important consideration for interior landscaping. The selection of the interior plant size should be determined according to the place that it will be planted or located.

Plant materials may be categorised according to the following sizes. Large trees have 12 metres height or more. Intermediate trees, have a max height of 9-12 metres. Small trees and ornamentals, have a max of 4.5-6 metres height. Tall shrubs, has max height 3 metres. Intermediate shrubs are 2 metres height. Low shrubs are 1 metre or fewer in mature height. Ground covers are used to describe any low or spreading plant material that has max height of 15-30 centimetres. (Fasli, M., et al 2004)

Large trees are dominant visual elements and they are used for focal points. In interior spaces, for example shopping malls, they are usually used at the common spaces where there is high ceiling and they take the attraction of the viewers. Besides, they are used for dominancy and reduction of heights. Fig.2.16

Shrubs are generally used for outdoor spaces. For interior spaces, generally they are not preferred. However, in interior volumes, small shrubs are used for space definition and aesthetic. Ground covers are defined the edges of patterns on the ground plane. They can be used in a design to define non-walking surfaces. In interior spaces, they are not used very much. In shopping malls, they are sometimes used with other plant materials such as trees and shrubs and they create a compositional accent and aesthetic view.

Plant form
Form is one of the other visual plants characteristic to be discussed. The form of an individual plant or group of plants is the overall shape, or its silhouetted outline. Not as visually strong as size, plant form is nevertheless a key factor in establishing the formation of a plant composition, influencing unity and variety, acting as accents or backgrounds, and coordinating landscaping with the solid mass of other elements in the design.

Plant colour

Plant colour is present through different parts of the plant including foliage, flowers, fruit, twigs and branches and trunk bark. In foliage, the principal colour is of course green, with many variations from dark green to light green including shades of yellow, blue, and bronze.

Colour plants or trees in interior spaces, especially in shopping malls are generally used for aesthetic purposes or take people's attraction to a point. Fig.2.17

Fig.2.17 Red Bull Music Academy, designed by Langarita-Navarro Arquitectos, María Langarita and Víctor Navarro. Green is the principle colour of the project, with a rich variation from light green, grass green, dark green, to breen.

Fig.2.16 Orona Hernani, designed by LUR PAISAJISTAK S.L.. Large palm trees are placed in the spacious interior with wooden benches on the side where people can rest. The small and ornamental trees are used as a foreground to focal point and they may serve as a visual and compositional accent because of their flowers.

Foliage type

As a design element, foliage plants can soften the look of an interior space and help to cover architectural defects; a specimen tree or plant grouping could visually separate an open-plan living and dining area, for instance, or the height of a high ceiling could be reduced by using hanging plants. In general, deciduous plants are not preferred for interior space and shopping malls. On the other hand, artificial coniferous evergreen (pine trees) are preferred for Christmas and New Year time for decoration.

2.5.2 Interior décor and furnishing

Interior décor and furnishing includes, plant container, interior decoration elements, furnishing and etc. In the following sections more information will be given about these.

Plant container

The pots that the plants are planted inside are called plant container. The containers for indoor and outdoor plants add aesthetic qualities to a landscape design. The containers could be in various shapes like cylinder, half cylinder, square, rectangle, tier and topsider. For interior spaces, metal, wrought iron and steel container can be used. The container height can be short or tall that are arrange according to the plant size. They are covered with different colors like brown, white, black, bronze, metallic and etc. The containers are made of several finishes, including ceramic and plastic square planters that shine with a metallic finish.

Furnishing

Furnishings complete interior designs, like landscaping do. Indoor plants and containers act as the main components of a landscaping.

The interior furnishing includes, sitting elements, dust bins and advertisement boards etc. They are used for both comfort and aesthetical purposes. Sitting elements could be from timber (wood), concrete or leather coverings etc. On the other hand, dust bins are generally metal and wood covered, statues are from stone or metal. All are used for both aesthetical and functional purposes.

Arbor	Bush	Herbaceous
Ficus Benjamina	Euphorbia pulcherrima	Impatiens spp.
Bucida buceras	Epipremnum aureum	Alocasia spp.
Washingtonaia robusta	Fatsia japonica	Nephrolepis exaltataspp.
Livisona chinensisrobusta	Cycas revoluta	Aglaonema
Podocarpus gracillior Veitcha merillii Bambusa vulgaris aereo−variegatus		Spathiphyllum
Ficus nitida		Hedera canariensis
Phyllostachys aurea Clusia rosea Dracaena marginata Dracaena reflexa Beaucarnea recurvata Phyllostachys nigra'Henon' Cyrtomium falcatum		Moraea iridoides
Magnolia grandiflora Eucalyptus sideroxylon Jacaranda acutifolia Crytomeria japonica Pandanus veitchii Chamaedorea elegans		Pittosporum tobira
Ptychosperma elegans Ficus pumila		Cissus antarctica
Gardenia jasmanoides Syagrus romanzoffianum		Dieffenbachia
Caryota urens		Ficus pumila
		Helxine soleirolii
		Ophiopogon japonicus
		Neoregelia spp.
		Pepperomia fosteri Liriope spp.
		Aspidistra elatior Dendrobium spp. Ardisia crispa Cyrtomium falcatum
		Asplenium nidus Calathea zebrina
		Aeschynanthus lobbianus
		Eucharis grandiflora
		Codiaeum sp.
		Cyperus papyrus
		Strelitzia nicolai
		Syngonium podophylum Zamia furfuracea

Chapter Three

The Making of Interior Landscape

3.1 Growing Media

A wide variety of growing media are used by interior landscapers. They all have their advantages and faults and it is quite a complex science to work out which growing medium works best in different situations.

Growing media is a broad term covering a multitude of mixtures that the plants grow in. Often called soil or compost (or dirt in North America), the materials used have to perform a surprisingly wide range of functions.

3.1.1 Functions of growing media

The growing medium has many functions. It must provide a suitable anchorage for the plant's roots; it must act as a reservoir for water and nutrients; it acts as a buffer against sudden changes in the environment, especially changes in temperature and, for indoor plants in containers, it must be sufficiently heavy to provide stability to the plant display and reduce the risk of it toppling over.

Anchorage

Plant roots grow into the growing medium to extract nutrients and water, but they also serve to anchor the plant into the ground to prevent it from falling over. Often the texture of the growing medium determines how well the roots can ramify through it.

Water

A well-structured growing medium acts as a reservoir for the water a plant needs. Indoor plant displays are often fitted with subterranean irrigation systems that supply water to the growing medium, but it is the water in the growing medium around the plant roots that acts as the plant's primary source of water.

The texture of the growing medium affects the rate at which water is absorbed and the volume that can be held. This is an important consideration for keepers of indoor plants where different species have very different requirements.

Nutrients

Fertiliser is usually applied to the growing medium before it can be extracted by the plant roots. The chemical composition of the growing medium has a dramatic effect on the uptake of fertilizer nutrients. Media with a high clay content can lock up certain nutrients whereas loamless media, such as peat, are less able to bind nutrient chemicals resulting in greater demand of those nutrients to the plants.

Stability

Many indoor plants are displayed in freestanding containers. Often the height of the plant is more than four times the diameter of its container so, unless the container and the growing medium are sufficiently heavy, there is a risk that the plant display may be unstable.

3.1.2 Types of growing media

The growing media can be divided into the following types:

Peat-based media

Peat forms the basis of many growing media used in interior landscapes. There are many reasons for its popularity, but there are also environmental concerns that need to be addressed.

Peat is a natural product formed by the partial decomposition of mosses and sedges. The decomposition occurs in acid, waterlogged conditions where the micro-organisms that would normally break down.

The good reasons of peat are:
- Good structure and texture, which encourages root development.
- Good water holding capacity without getting too waterlogged which makes it ideal for use with subterranean irrigation systems.
- Good chemical properties making fertiliser application easy. There are no minerals that will lock up nutrients, so fertilizer rates can be low. Soil pH can be adjusted so that nutrient uptake is always optimal.
- Gore or less sterile, so there is little risk of soil-borne plant diseases.
- Lightweight, so plant displays are easy to transport and move once in situ.

- Most plants are already grown in peat-based mixtures, so there is little risk of transplant shock when plant displays are planted up into landscape containers. The plants are already adapted to their environment.
- Supplies from reputable companies means that there are good quality assurance procedures in place to ensure that the product is consistent.
- A natural product so very little product processing is required.

There are many different types of peat. The differences are related to the environment under which the decomposition took place, the types of moss and sedge that decomposed and the time since the decomposition started. Whilst there are a multitude of ways to classify peat, many horticulturists refer to sedge peat (dark and very decomposed with a fine texture) and sphagnum peat (derived from the upper layers of peat bogs, paler in color and with a discernible structure). Sphagnum peat is the type usually found in growing media used by interior landscapers.

However, in many countries, especially the UK, there are concerns that the use of peat by gardeners and horticulturists is damaging the environment. This is because some peat is extracted from moors that form unique ecosystems and support a very special range of plants and animals.

Peat-based growing media usually contain other ingredients. Peat alone is not ideal. In the UK, peat-based growing media often include some grit to provide extra weight and some inert particles, such as perlite, to aid aeration. Ground limestone is often added to raise the PH to between 5.5 and 6.5.

Outside of the UK, peat-based media often contain additional components such as composted wood fibre and bark. A common mixture used in New Zealand also contains as much as 50% pumice extracted from the volcanic debris found there.

Alternatives to peat
There are now many alternatives to peat as components of growing me-

dia. Some are better suited for use in interior landscapes than others. The most common alternatives include bark, coir, wood-based products, organic waste and spent mushroom compost.

Bark

Composted bark is now a common component of many growing media. It has the advantage of being both a waste product from other processes and a completely renewable resource. However, there are some inherent difficulties that need to be overcome when using bark-based media.

The most important characteristic of bark-based mixtures is its decomposition by fungi in the mixture. This process uses a lot of nitrogen, which can result in deficiency for the plant. This decomposition can also result in elevated temperatures and the growth of mushrooms on the surface of the medium. This is unacceptable in indoor plant displays and is the main reason why bark-based media are not popular among interior landscapers.

Bark used in growing media comes from both softwood and hardwood sources. Softwood bark, from species such as the Scots pine and spruce, is rich in phosphorus, calcium and potassium.

Hardwood bark must be thoroughly composted before it is incorporated into growing media. This is because it is toxic to plants in its raw state. However, hardwood bark has been shown to be able to suppress some damaging soil fungi and root-destroying nematodes (eelworms).

Coir

Coir is a by-product of the coconut industry. It is made from the ground husks and fibrous shells of coconuts and is now very popular. Like bark, coir is a waste product and comes from a renewable source, so there are environmental benefits. However, coir has not yet proved popular amongst interior landscapers.

The benefits of coir include:
- Good structure and texture. Coir encourages root development and has good water holding capacity without getting too waterlogged. It is ideal for use with subterranean irrigation systems.

- Coir has good chemical properties making fertiliser application easy. There are no minerals that will lock up nutrients, so fertiliser application rates can be low. Soil PH can be adjusted so that nutrient uptake is always optimal.
- Coir is more or less sterile, so there is little risk of soil-borne plant diseases.
- Coir is lightweight, so plant displays are easy to transport and move once in situ.
- Coir is clean and sterile, so few risks of soil-borne plant diseases.

However, there are some disadvantages:
Variable quality and consistency of product. This is because the coir has often been left exposed to the elements before being processed. This is less of a problem now than it was a few years ago when it was first introduced.

Coir has to be transported from Sri Lanka, so the environmental benefits gained from using a renewable product have to be compared with the environmental disadvantages of shipping a product around the world.

The raw material needs processing before the product can be used. The environmental benefits of using a renewable product have to be compared with the environmental disadvantages of additional industrial processing.

Plants suitable for coir will have been grown in peat and will have peat compost in the root ball, so it will be impossible to guarantee a totally peat-free plant display.

Wood-based products
Some manufacturers now include wood-based products (other than bark) in growing media. These include sawdust and ground wood chips. These products have many of the disadvantages of bark with the additional risk that wood that has been treated with timber preservatives may be included. These may be toxic to plants.

Loam and soil-based media

Loam or soil-based media are less common in interior landscapes than peat-based media. They are often heavy and difficult to handle and, as they are made from soil, consistency is difficult to maintain.

Some growing media are produced that contain a mixture of peat and soil. These include the famous John Innes compost mixtures that are formulated for specific horticultural purposes.

Many interior landscapes featuring large trees use media including some loam. This is to provide greater stability and anchorage for the trees.

3.2 Irrigation Systems

Watering plants is the single most time-consuming part of the service technician's job. It is also boring and wastes the time of our skilled staff. For this reason, several companies have developed what they consider to be a panacea – the ultimate irrigation system.

3.2.1 Different types of irrigation systems

There are several different categories of irrigation systems, such as self-contained subterranean irrigation, semi-hydro subterranean irrigation, electronically controlled built-in systems, and hydroculture.

Self-contained subterranean irrigation

These systems are very popular. There are also many different products available. One look at any issue of "Interiorscape" magazine or in an Interior landscape supplies catalogue will show just how many of these systems there are. Most subterranean irrigation systems operate in the same way. A tank of water is placed in the soil, under the plant, and water is drawn into the soil through wicks or soil plugs by means of capillarity. Good examples include the well-known "Mona" system, the "Rentokil Irrigation System" and the "Tanker" system.

Semi-hydro subterranean irrigation

Semi-hydro subterranean irrigation is very popular in many European countries. It is a very simple, cheap and effective method of watering plants, although setting up the system can be a little tricky. The bottom few centimetres of a container are filled with LECA (Light Expanded Clay

Aggregate) granules. On this, a layer of capillary matting is laid. Capillary wicks are sometimes fixed to the bottom of the mat to trail into the LECA layer. Ordinary potting compost is then added to fill the remainder of the container. A filler tube is included that runs from the soil surface to the LECA layer. The LECA layer acts as a sump and reservoir for irrigation water.

The plant is then planted into the compost as normal and installed on site. To begin with, the plant is top-watered as well as having water added to the LECA layer. Once the roots of the plant have grown sufficiently, watering via the filler tube into the LECA layer is all that is necessary.

There are two main disadvantages to this system.
First, if this system is used with ceramic containers, the container must be lined or made completely waterproof. This can increase preparation time and add to complexity.
The second drawback is that there is a body of free water in the container, not held in a separate tank. This means that even the slightest crack in the container could result in a leak.

3.2.2 The benefits of subterranean irrigation
Most systems allow an increased interval between watering, sometimes to as much as four to six weeks. Subterranean irrigation reduces the risk of sciarid fly infestation. This is because sciarid flies (fungus gnats) can only breed in the top few centimetres of the soil, which has to be damp. Subterranean irrigation keeps the soil surface dry at all times. A dry soil surface also reduces the risk of soil fungi. Plant longevity is increased. Experiments have shown that plants live longer, grow bigger and look better when subterranean irrigation is used. Subterranean irrigation allows the use of a wider range of decorative top-dressings that would otherwise be washed into the soil by top watering.

3.3 Temperature and Humidity

Most indoor plants are tropical or subtropical in origin. This means that they are already quite well adapted to the temperatures found in most buildings. Another feature of the tropical parts of the world is the lack of seasonal variation compared with more temperate areas. This is important because the indoor environment of most buildings is also fairly constant throughout the year, which again means that tropical plants will be well adapted to conditions indoors.

Although the amounts of water and light available to a plant are the most important factors governing its survival indoors, a plant's health and appearance may also be affected by the nature of the air around it. Extremes of temperature and humidity, or the presence of pollutant dust and fumes can be very damaging to the leaves and encourage pests, diseases and disorders.

3.3.1 Temperature

In most buildings, the temperature is quite uniform and suitable for a wide range of plants. There are, however, a few situations where the temperature can be more extreme and care must be taken to install only plant species that will tolerate the conditions, or to avoid installing live plants altogether.

Too hot

Aside from cacti and succulents, most indoor plants find it difficult to cope with excessively hot conditions. The rate at which water transpires from the leaves may exceed the rate at which it can be taken in by the roots, even if the growing medium is very moist. This may cause the plant to wilt, lose leaves and suffer permanent cell damage. Such hot, dry conditions also favour the spread of plant pests, such as Two-spotted (red) spider mite, Tetranychus urticae.

Particular care must be taken to avoid putting plants close to south-facing windows in summer. The sun is likely to scorch the leaves; the same is likely to occur if the plant is too close to a radiator or hot air intake.

Too cold

Aside from frost, which is lethal to most indoor plants, cold is generally tolerated better by plants than heat. Draughts and sudden changes in temperature can cause leaf drop, but provided the plant is given the opportunity to acclimatize and is not over-watered, it can survive surprisingly well in very chilly environments.

The point about acclimatisation is an important one to remember when moving plants around a building. Suddenly moving a plant from one temperature to another e.g. a warm office to a draughty corridor or vice versa, is likely to shock it into losing a lot of leaves.

3.3.2 Humidity

Despite being an essential ingredient of photosynthesis, only 1%-2% of the water entering a plant is used for that purpose. The remainder evaporates from the surface of the leaves by transpiration, which increases with light levels and temperature. It also varies with humidity, which can be quite variable in buildings.

Diffusion of water from the moisture-laden air spaces of the leaf to the outside goes on rather slowly when the surrounding air is humid. However, when the surrounding air is dry, diffusion and thus the transpiration rate are increased. In extreme cases the leaves may wilt, because the roots cannot take in enough water to keep pace with the rate of water loss. Other problems associated with low humidity are brown leaf edges and tips, and a higher incidence of pests such as Two-spotted (red) spider mite, Tetranychus urticae.

3.3.3 Pollutants

Plants may be damaged if their environment contains excessive amounts of dust, fumes or another pollutants. In particular:
- Dust on the upper surface of the leaves reduces the amount of light reaching the plant
- Grease and grime may block the breathing pores (stomata), which allow air and moisture transfer in the leaves.

3.4 Top Dressings

3.4.1 Why use top dressings?

In the bad old days, top dressings weren't needed. That is because interior landscapers thought it would be a good idea to stuff ugly containers with so many plants that the soil could not be seen. Luckily, those days are gone and we now tend to make use of single characterful specimens in good quality containers. Often, the plants have trunks and the soil surface is left exposed.

3.4.2 Why not appropriate to me top dressings?

Firstly, and most importantly, it is ugly. Unless the soil surface is constantly refreshed and tidied, it soon looks tired. If the plants are top watered, you end up with damp and dry patches and hollows where a torrent of water hit the surface.

Secondly, it accumulates rubbish. Dead leaves and office litter often find their ways onto the soil surface, which is difficult to keep tidy.

Thirdly, the soil surface is where fungus gnats (sciarid flies) breed. If you can stop them getting there, then you will not have a problem with them.

3.4.3 Types of top dressings

There are dozens of different materials that are used to cover the surface of the soil in a container. The most common are bark, gravel (Fig.3.1), cobblestones and Spanish moss. These four materials probably make up

Fig.3.1 Vitrea Suite, designed by Alberto Apostoli. The substrate is sphagnum moss.

over 75% of the top dressings used worldwide. More recently, however, a wide range of new products have become available. These include:

Recycled glass chippings
Crushed sea shells (sometimes dyed)
"Coffee beans" – spray painted gravel in many colours
Marble chippings
Slate chippings
Mock bark, made from recycled car tyres, often in different colours
Chipped quartz and other semi-precious minerals.

3.4.4 Factors that affect the choice of top dressing

The most important factor to affect the choice of top dressing is how it looks with the plant and the container. Sometimes, a contrast between a dark container and a pale dressing looks really good. However, the dressing should never overwhelm the plant, especially if it doesn't have a defined trunk. Fig.3.2.

Modern containers look best with a contemporary dressing. Polished or brushed metal, especially silver, looks very good with glass or marble chippings. Older, more traditional containers benefit from the use of older, more traditional dressings, e.g. bark or moss. One other very important factor to consider is how the plant display is watered.

3.4.5 Top dressings to avoid

Heavy cobbles, as these compact the soil and will shorten the life of the plants. Heavy cobbles may also destabilise the display and the plant may lean to one side. These should also be avoided in public places such as shopping centres where unruly children may throw them around and cause damage.

Wood chips unless they have been sterilised and made fire retardant. Unsterilised wood chips may rot and encourage the growth of fungi and provide a habitat for Sciarid flies (Fungus gnats).

Fig.3.2 Vitrea Suite, designed by Alberto Apostoli. The substrate is sphagnum moss, a natural plant product.

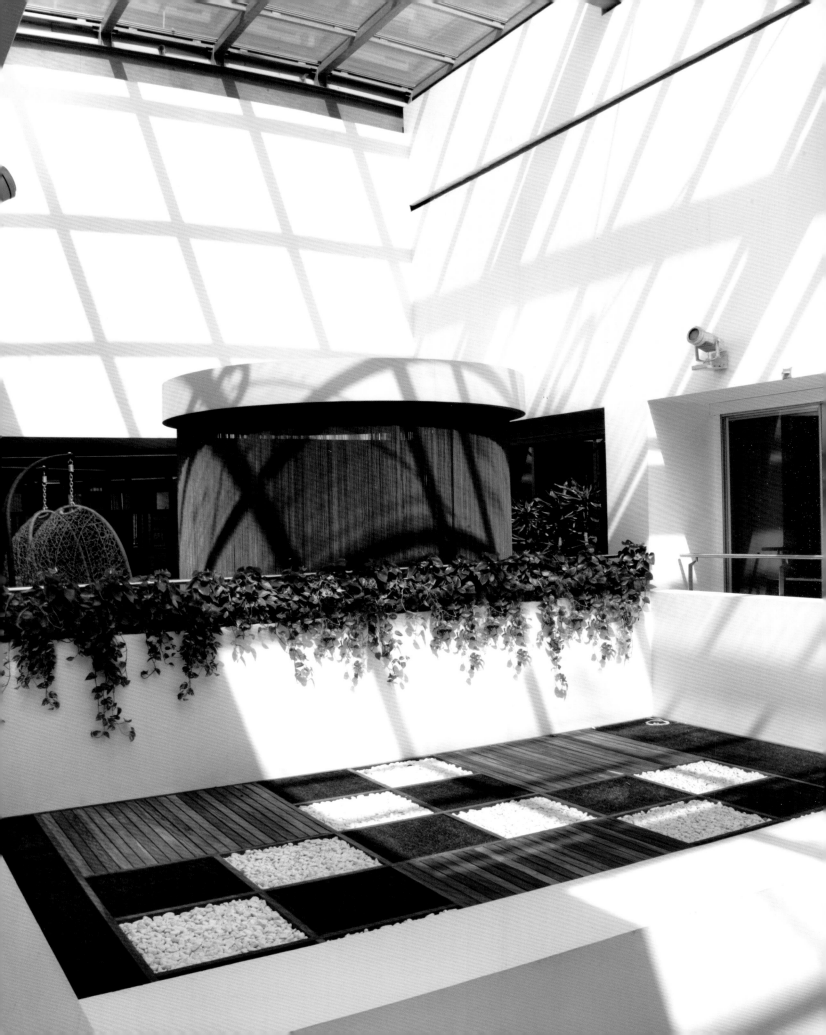

Chapter Four

Landscape Design of Atriums

Because atriums are so complex, they create unique interrelationships between spaces in the architecture. Typical atrium configurations can be totally surrounded by building elements or partially enclosed. They maybe top lit, side lit or a combination of both. Fig.4.1 to 4.3

Good atrium design will maximise the natural environment to minimise energy consumption, in which plants, water and other natural elements plays an important part. Fig.4.4

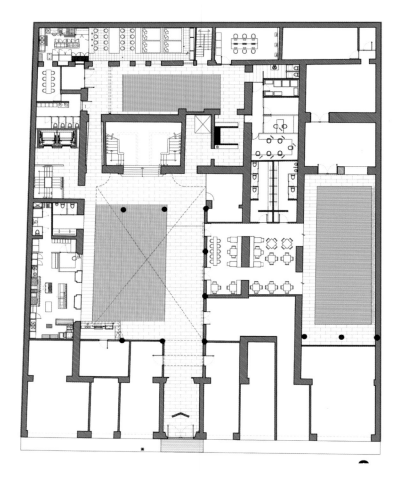

Fig.4.1 to 4.3 Hotel Centro, designed by CHEREMSERRANO. The ground floor has two other inner courtyards which separate the spaces and surround the corridors resembling an Hacienda. The patios are the main distributors of space, allowing natural light and ventilation into the hotel and consequently decreasing the use of energy, artificial light and air conditioning.

Fig.4.4 The IBC Innovation Factory by schmidt hammer lassen architects is designed to support new ways of learning. The main task for schmidt hammer lassen architects has been to preserve and emphasise the building's existing qualities and transform the facilities into an innovative learning environment. By using six elements – fire, water, greenery, light, sound and air – the concept for the new Innovation Factory was developed with an emphasis on stimulating the users' senses.

INRA Research Laboratories in Champenoux

Behind its light appearance, this building hides the high technical standards required by its brief. The architects and the client worked together in mutually-beneficial symbiosis to optimise its performance and to involve the entire local timber industry in a highly relevant way.

Completion date:
2013
Location:
Nancy, France
Designer:
Tectoniques
Landscape designer:
Itinéraire Bis
Photographer:
Renaud Araud
Area:
1,440 sqm

Project Description:

The Champenoux site in the Lorraine region is one of the five sites of the Institut National de la Recherche Agronomique (National Agronomic Research Institute) in France. Located in the immense forest of Amance, it has added a new laboratories and offices building on the existing site.

These high-level technical research centres host French and foreign researchers who work together to study the ecology and genomics of forests. Due to its history and its geographical position, the INRA centre in Nancy has always been largely devoted to the study of the forest and its products (of which timber is the most important). Five hundred people study

subjects from the genome to the territory, including the functioning of trees and of ecosystems, as well as the forestry economy and the production of biomass.

For these specialists of timber in France, the scheme had to be exemplary from an environmental viewpoint, with a clearly-visible "all wood" character, in order to make the building's form consistent with its function.

Its curved south façade encompasses the site's entire entrance and appears like a series of strips of timber on a landscape background. The smooth north side is a response to the other buildings which date from the 1960s. These two dynamic elements of the

scheme are linked by an atrium, which is the real heart of the scheme.

Main features:
- Experimental wood-fired boiler using miscanthus grown, gathered and prepared on the site by INRA
- Timber structural framework construction in "Sélection Vosges" solid fir / 600 m^3 of timber
- Air-ground heat exchanger
- Thick external walls with triple glazing (except wall facing south)
- Central atrium with natural air draught and ventilation

The atrium, between a nerve centre and an indoor garden

The atrium is the scheme's nerve centre. It is like the inside of a "bee-hive" that thrives on the mutual visibility between the various activities. It is a place for interaction, discussion, sharing and encounters, for exhibitions of work. This image transforms our perception of research. It connects the two buildings in a pleasant atmosphere characterised by the interplay of stairs, catwalks and transparent views.

To stress the unique character of this space, the landscapers of the Itinéraire Bis firm designed an exotic garden with a different, surprising nature that is tropicalised, abundant and colourful.

All the circulation areas, stairs and lifts are immersed in this indoor landscape. The atrium is generously lit, watered with recovered rainwater. It features an attractive pool, and it is planted directly into the ground. Plants are organised in three strata: herbaceous plants on the

1. The atrium

ground, shrubs and bushes up to human height, and large column-shaped trees that go up through the floor levels.

"The principle was that the plantations illustrate all the strata of the tropical rain forest, both linked to the subject of some of the Institute's researchers and in response to the temperature and humidity conditions in the atrium. Each stratum is characterised by a representative plant (ground cover plant: creeping dwarf fig-tree, shrub: bird of paradise; climbing plant/liana or vine: star jasmine; epiphyte plant: candelabra aloes; tree: jaggery palm [Caryota urens]; aquatic plant: giant horsetail)."

For the experts of local forests, it is an unusual exotic wooded habitat, compatible with heat that is maintained constant all year.

Thanks to the atrium, the two north and south strips which are occupied by spaces of low depth – have double aspects, with the known advantages in terms of views, ventilation and daylighting. The large dished membrane of ETFE plastic that covers it provides uniform, diffuse controlled natural light, producing an artificial sky effect.

Double-sided building
The accommodation is separated into two sides. The north side of the scheme is a response to the existing 1960s buildings on the site, with a smooth facade, facings of bakelized panels, and horizontal strips of windows. It echoes the buildings that look onto them, to which it is linked by a timber access balcony. Most of the laboratories are on this side of the building; they benefit from stable light, with no overheating in summer, and they keep a direct visual connection with the rest of the Campus.

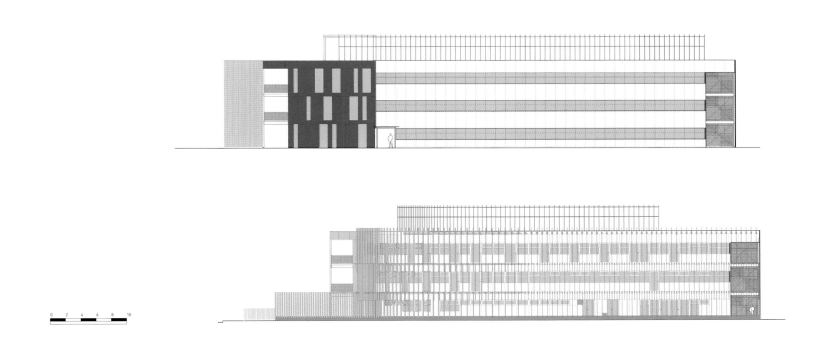

The south side materialises the Campus entrance. It characterizes the scheme with its double skin of wood and its curved plan. Most of the offices are on this side of the building, clearly visible on the entrance road, fitted with appropriate solar protection, and benefiting from long-distance views.

The external access balconies, protected by a timber claustra, extend the work spaces by creating a play of timber strips and of interwoven or criss-crossed horizontal and vertical strips. The access balconies act as canopies, adjusted to balance solar protection and solar gains and to protect the necessary privacy and confidentiality. The density varies according to the aspect. From East to West, the texture of the outer "skin" densifies and creates a dynamic effect on the façade.

The guard rails in stainless steel grid and the metal grating floors bring lightness and transparency to this outer skin, creating numerous weaving effects. It is a suspended, independent structure in order to avoid heat bridges, constructed according to the principle of using one single timber cross-section (4 cm x 12 cm) throughout, in order to maintain a very fine appearance.

Revealed structure

Outside a technical area on the ground floor of the north building, the entire scheme is in timber structure, which is a first time for a complex of laboratories with such high technical requirements (regarding temperature, pollution, vibrations, etc.).

Timber is used everywhere (for façades, floors and internal partition walls). Above and beyond arguments in

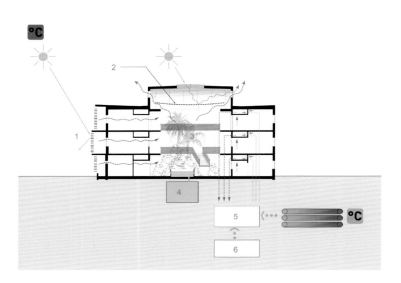

1. The building is fitted with a solar protection system.
2. The ETFE inner roof over the atrium helps balance the atmosphere inside.
3. Evaporation treatment
4. Rainwater is recovered in an underground tank.
5. Double air exchange
6. The battery in PAC helps in cooling water.

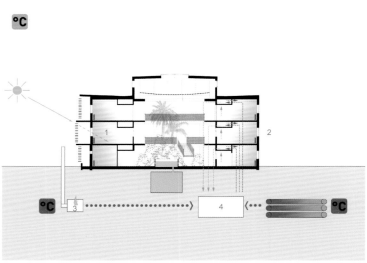

1. Solar heating system
2. Triple glazing
3. Wood–fired boiler
4. Double air exchange

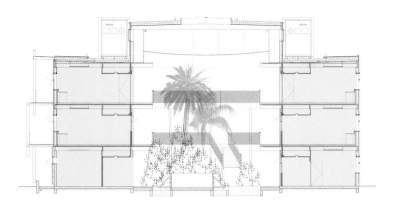

Section on the atrium

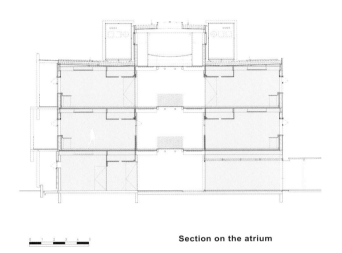

Section on the atrium

favour of eco-construction, which Tectoniques promotes in all its projects, it echoes the subject of research conducted in these laboratories (into forest genomics).

The chosen construction scheme consists in using solid timber elements with small spans and closely spaced on a 1.20 m x 6 m construction grid. It is a scheme that uses a lot of local timber selected from the adjacent forest which is converted or processed very little.

The dry construction, the use of short-span structural grids, the size and means of assembly of the prefabricated "macro-components", and a plan that is easy to extend are all measures that ensure the future adaptability of this laboratory building, including in the short term. The floor spaces are freed of any structures, and they can be partitioned and modified as desired according to needs.

Considering this very visible construction system, one can say that this project is very representative of the work of the Tectoniques firm. One may draw a parallel, for example, with the Espace Nordique for the Biathlon in Bessans (in the Savoie area of the French Alps).

Experimenting with timber from a short production-marketing-distribution channel

This scheme highlights and promotes the qualities of wood: 250 m^3 of silver fir and Douglas fir were used for this project, only in the form of solid timber. It is an illustration of the potential of the region's forest and timber industry to meet very specific demand. The timber used for structural purposes was obtained from forests of the Vosges mountains, in which the trees were chosen while standing for their dimensional and mechanical characteristics. The timber was sawn just a few kilometres from the construction site and it supplied according to a standard contract put in place in recent years by the ONF (National Forests Office).

This promotes Vosges fir, while even the large and very large softwoods which characterise the forests of the Vosges mountain range pose problems of outlets. Seasoned and planed C24 classified structural timber (with CE marking) of the Sélection Vosges brand, was used. It was decided to use back-sawn (tangentially cut) timber, which required special know-how that is specific to sawmills of the Lorraine region. The Bastien sawmill in Romoneix carried out the operation using logs from the State forest of Ormont-Robache forest and from the Défilé de Straiture ravine. Close cooperation was established between ONF and the sawmill: all wood used for the INRA building is completely traceable.

Specific facilities

A certain number of measures are applied to obtain exemplary environmental quality, associated with French NF HQE (High Environmental Quality) certification for service sector and office buildings:

The first measure concerns the performance of the building envelope: very thick wood-wool insulation and triple glazing (except for parts facing south).

An air-ground heat exchanger, constructed with the precau¬tions required for a swelling clay soil, provides preheated or cooled air.

An experimental wood-fired boiler was installed as a complement to the site's existing gas-fired boiler. It uses miscanthus, which is grown, gathered and prepared on

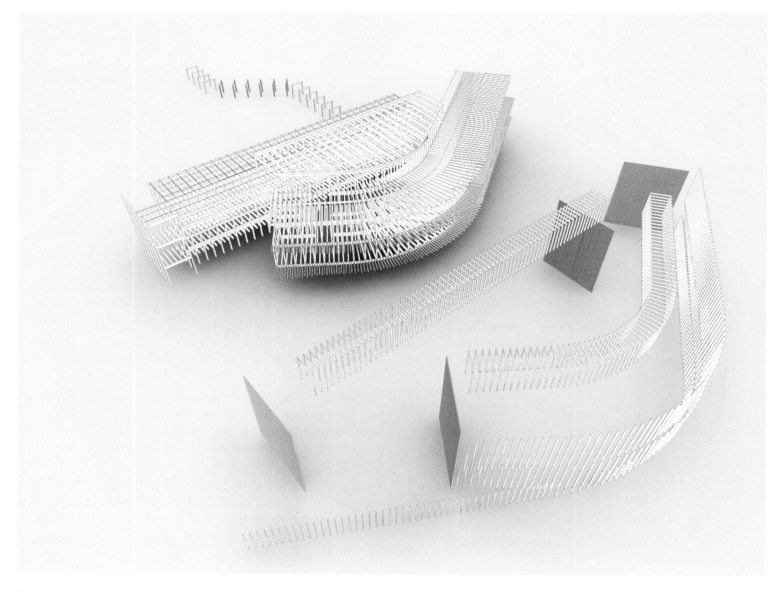

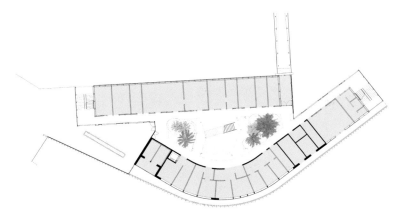

Plan of the ground floor

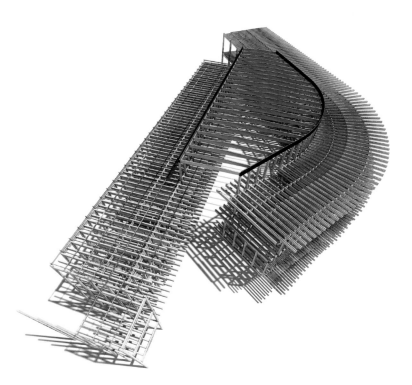

1. The interior façade

the site by INRA, as a complement to wood chips. A shed was built, as part of the project, for storing it.

The atrium, covered by a dished ETFE inner roof composed of 3 membranes, creates a draught of air. In winter, the system is moderated by overhead solar gain and by the floor heating system. In summer, automated openers provide natural ventilation of the premises.

A fume chambers system complements the natural systems for meeting the laboratories' requirements. It occupies a services floor level that sits on top of the building, from which it is separated, bearing on plots and on insulation.

Rainwater recovered in an underground tank is used for the pools in the indoor garden, for the toilets and for watering the plants.

Herringbone Restaurant

In addition to visual playfulness, the design provides a sensually lush atmosphere, converting an industrial warehouse into an indoor olive grove. This verdant ambience is further infused with aged, natural textures and earth-toned colours and light.

Completion date:
2012
Location :
California, USA
Design Company:
Schoos Design
Designers:
Thomas Schoos, Jaime Sartwell
Photographer:
Matthew Hutchison
Area:
557 sqm

Project Description:

One of the main design challenges that Thomas Schoos faced when creating Herringbone Restaurant in La Jolla, California was to convert a cold, dark warehouse into an inviting environment for fresh California cuisine. One of the key ways Schoos accomplished this goal was to fill the space with an indoor olive grove, bringing six 100-year-old trees inside the restaurant. The presence of these huge natural wonders truly transforms the space, allowing guests to enjoy the sight of the trees' ancient, gnarled trunks, as well as the dappled light from overarching branches. However, achieving this goal required considerable effort and planning to accommodate the needs of these delicate living organisms. In fact, the planning had to begin six months in advance in order to prepare the trees for transplantation. Olive trees have very wide and shallow root systems that allow them to optimise the limited water available in arid climates. This is especially true for olive trees as old as the ones chosen for Herringbone. It would be impossible to capture the entire root system, or even a majority of it, during the transplantation process.

In order to uproot such large trees safely, the process began by gradually pruning the roots to allow the trees to adjust to a more constrained environment. First, the roots in the upper layer were cut to a depth of about 24 inches at a distance of 8 feet from the trunk. The tree was then allowed to sit undisturbed for two to three months so that it could "heal" and adjust to the loss of its roots. Then,

another cut was made to the roots at a depth of 12 additional inches, angling inward toward the centre. The tree was then allowed to sit undisturbed for two to three more months for more healing and adjusting. Only then were the trees removed from the ground and the roots wrapped for shipping.

Only two trees will fit onto a tractor-trailer truck, so, three trucks were required to transport the six trees to the restaurant. Meanwhile, inside the restaurant, six holes 10 feet by 10 feet wide and 7 feet deep were dug into the earth beneath the floor. The trees, with their root systems measuring 8 feet by 8 feet, were installed into the holes, along with a special mix of soil and a subterranean irrigation system that allows for automatic watering on a weekly basis. On the floor of the restaurant, metal grates measuring 8 feet by 8 feet surround each tree trunk, allowing air to flow through the holes, as well as providing access for periodic testing of the soil for proper moisture and nutrition. The root systems, of course, are once again free to spread into the earth below the restaurant as far as necessary.

Besides providing for a healthy root system, the atmosphere of the restaurant also had to be considered. Skylights were installed in the main dining room to provide enough light. Besides ample light, though, the trees require the proper mixture of moisture and air. To provide this, a "swamp cooler" (a type of natural air conditioning that uses water to cool the air so that it is moist instead of dry) is turned on every night and allowed to run until morning so that the trees get several hours of cool, fresh, moist air to compensate for the periods of heat and dryness preferred by humans.

In the front portion of the restaurant, Schoos decided to enhance the indoor/outdoor effect even further by tearing the roof off the building completely, leaving the walls intact, as well as the arched steel structure that formerly supported the roof. This created a large open courtyard that is used as a bar and lounge. This courtyard is inhabited by two of the six olive trees, which greet the guests and provide shade during the day. To mitigate the cool breezes from the nearby Pacific Ocean, Schoos added fireplaces

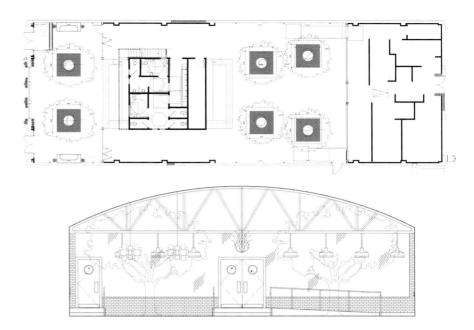

Plan drawing of the restaurant

1. Front courtyard with the overhead retractable awnings closed
2. View of main dining room with Beluga whale skeleton chandelier (foreground), olive trees and kitchen behind glass (rear)

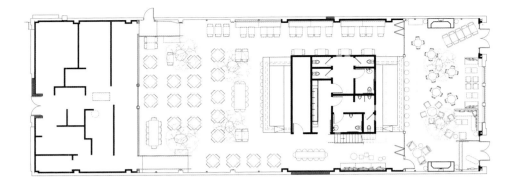

1. Main dining room
2. Inverted rowboat chandeliers, original paintings and olive trees
3. Close-up of an olive tree trunk and floor grate
4. The wall of stacked lobster traps filled with inflated puffer fish

on each end of the courtyard. He also decided to use the arched steel trusses that held the old barrel-shaped roof as the framework for a retractable awning system. At night, an electric pulley system draws canvas awnings closed over the lounge area, using the arched trusses as a track. This creates an atmosphere similar to a tent large enough to accommodate comfortable lounge furniture, full-grown trees and two fireplaces, with just a hint of fresh ocean air.

Besides the rich organic textures and atmosphere provided by these six large trees in the centre of the restaurant, Schoos made use of a number of other antique and natural textures to bring life to the interior of the restaurant and to remind guests of the nautical imagery associated with seafood. For instance, Schoos used antique wooden row boats to create a series of chandeliers, and created another dramatic chandelier from an entire whale skeleton suspended over the main bar inside a rustic steel framework

shaped like a blimp. Reclaimed wood, natural textures and nautical artifacts like corals and shells are featured prominently. And, for a whimsical art installation, an entire wall in the main dining room is filled with a stack of antique lobster traps full of inflated puffer fish with comical "google eyes". All of this goes together to create a theme for the restaurant that evokes California coastal living in an innovative way, while also providing a sensual indoor/outdoor atmosphere that is at once creative, comfortable and elegant.

Regional Printing House – a Bioclimatic Garden for an Office Building

This working space was facing an empty patio without vegetation that had the potential of being the bioclimatic core of the building.

Completion date:
2010
Location:
Apeldoorn, the Netherlands
Designer:
Ecoproyecta
Photographer:
David Frutos
Area:
208 sqm

Project Description:

In the south of Spain there are two problems that concern sustainable construction: water scarcity and high air conditioning demands. In the case of this particular building there was a problem of excess of solar radiation through the glass façades that produced overheating and discomfort for the workers.

On the other hand the promoters had planned an investment in solar energy. Ecoproyecta proposal was to consider all interventions as one integrated action. That means that the solar installation, the refurbishment of the building and the new garden were planned together as parts of a single project. The works

concluded in March 2010 giving as a result a more sustainable and comfortable building.

The main strategy was to cover the patio with a photovoltaic pergola that provided not only solar energy but also shading for the patio and all the offices facing it. The PV pergola was also designed to collect rain water and drive it to an underground water tank. This supply is used to water the garden and also to create a microclimate with nebulizers. So these were the perfect conditions (rain water, shade, humidity) to create a Mediterranean riverside ecosystem with native species, some fruit trees and some aromatic carpet plants.

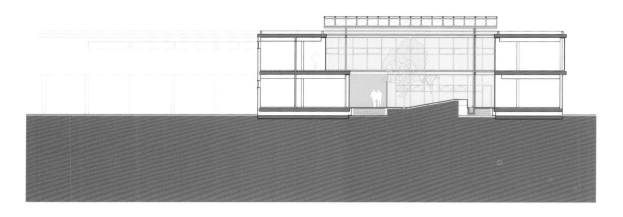

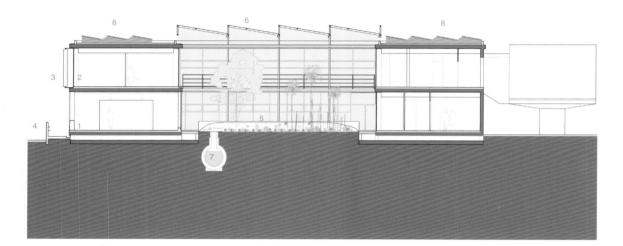

Cross Section
1. New customer service office
2. Refurbished second floor
3. Motorized louvers
4. Main access
5. Inside garden with native species
6. Photovoltaic pergola which collects solar energy and rain water
7. Underground rain water tank (20m³)
8. Solar panels creating ventilated roof

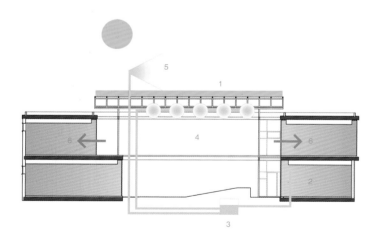

Sunny and warm days
1. Energy production through PV pergola
2. Collection of air cooling system condensation water
3. Water tank for sprinklers and nebulisers
4. Nebulisers to condition the patio microclimate
5. Top sprinklers to wash solar panels
6. Cool air ventilation through offices thanks to nebulisers and shades of the pergola. It is also a scented air from native aromatic plants

Rainy days
1. Collection of rain water from the pergola and conduction through pipes to tank
2. Rain water pond previous to tank
3. Underground tank stores rain water (20m³)
4. Sprinklers under pergola to water the garden
5. Rain water curtain creates sound and helps microclimate

Thus solar energy, bioclimatic strategies and landscape design were thought all together to create a garden that works as the new core of the building, providing cool ventilation, natural aromatic air and the nice sound of a fountain.

The project has won five awards so far. It is worth to point out these three: the Regional Energy Agency Prize, the Endesa second prize for the most sustainable building in Spain and the Spanish Solar Prize (by Eurosolar Association).

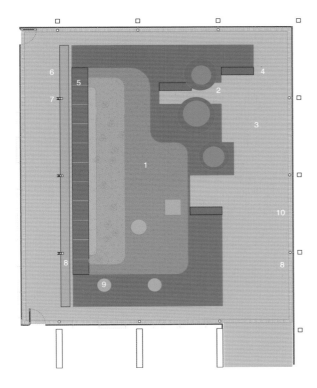

Garden Plan
1. Native carpet aromatic plants
2. Native fruit trees
3. Concrete paving
4. Concrete bench
5. Stone wall
6. Rain water pond
7. Steel pillar
8. Pipes to collect rain water
9. Underground tank for rain water
10. Perimeter ventilation grille

1. Rain water pond

Buyaka

"Shedding of Skin": The transformation of function is reflected formally in a gradual change of material. One material sheds another to become and say something else.

Completion date:
2012
Location:
Umraniye, Turkey
Designer:
Uras+Dilekci Architects
Photographer:
Faruk Kurtuluş, Ugur Ceylan
Area:
44,000 sqm

Project Description:

Buyaka is located in the Asian part of Istanbul, Ümraniye district. This district is one of the sub-centres of trade and residential zones.

Buyaka was designed without using a thematic overlay. The design approach portrays an honest intent to do with its programme as a mixed-use building. It attempts to reflect a sense of integrity with its formal language, emphasising that good design doesn't need thematic overlays.

In architecture, meaning and content has been transposed. We are living in an era where the authentic has lost its importance and has been overruled by the superficial and fake realities have become the norm. Fake, theatrical façades are applied to buildings without a relationship with function and programme. Materials mimic other materials with the excuse of cost effectiveness, creating a potpuri of postmodern clutter. What does the building say? Who is the user? It's an open question.

This potpuri of formal clutter has overtaken the fundamental role of architecture and architecture has become more of a pictorial race of artisans where origin and authentic notions have disintegrated.

Trying to design purposeless projects for developers without identified users has become a big challenge for architects. Amongst this conversation Buyaka stands at a place speak-

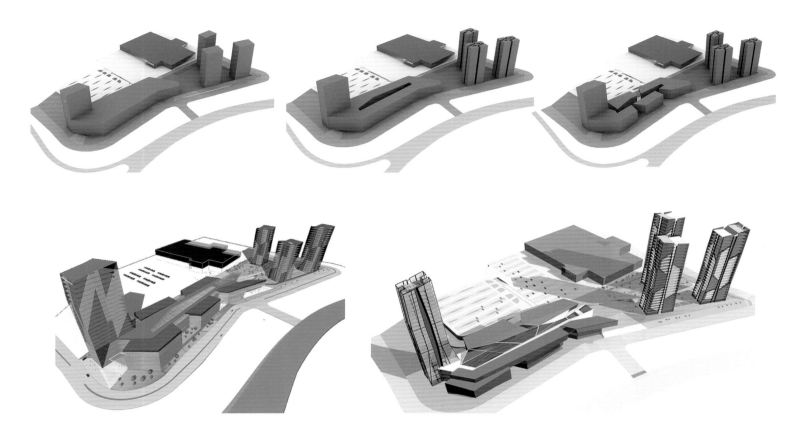

1. Lighting adds more charm to the pool

ing of architecture for the sake of architecture. It takes its references from itself and creates a formal dialogue unique to itself.

Concepts and Thoughts

Fragmentation: The main approach was to attempt to break the mega function boxes that are commonly seen in cities today into a more friendly and inviting formal language. The project consists of several horizontal and vertical prisms in dialogue with each other and their environment.

The play between dark dull surfaces and light shiny surfaces creates depth in the appearance of the building. The general black posture emphasises the contours of the building against the blue-gray Istanbul sky.

Speed: As the buildings are situated by a motorway junction, the perception of the building is cinematic. One mostly perceives the building by moving around it by car. This cinematic experience is cardiographed by play and juxtaposition of form and material.

Continuity: The structural dynamic is seamlessly reflected inside-out and outside-in, creating sculptural, glacier-like forms that speak with the fast moving surroundings.

Force projection: Buyaka is a power centre acting as a hub, taking impulses and also feeding the near environment without alienating itself, serving as a piece of the whole without getting lost in the popular identity crises of today.

Functions

Buyaka involves a shopping mall, three office buildings and a residential building. The shopping centre connects 21-storey office building with other two 23-storey office buildings and a 23-storey residential building with a unique atmosphere with its several prisms.

There are two kinds of main materials for façades. Composite panels were used for different types for the shopping center and glass curtain walls were used for different types for the office and residential buildings.

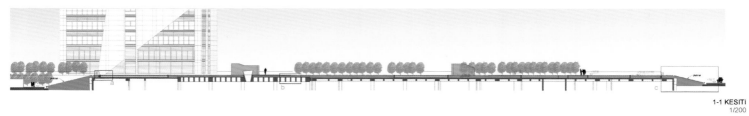

1-1 KESITI
1/200

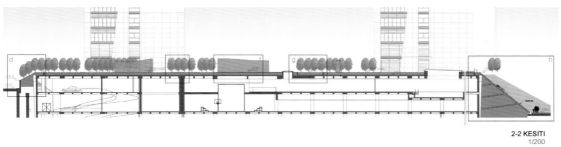

2-2 KESITI
1/200

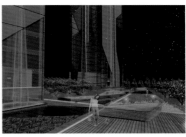

Layout Plan

1. A block office
2. Shopping centre
3. E block office
4. B block housing
5. C block office
6. A block entrance
7. Gym entrance
8. A block entrance
9. B block entrance
10. C block entrance
11. Shopping centre entrance
12. Service entrance
13. Shopping centre entrance
14. Parking entrance & exit
15. Indoor garden

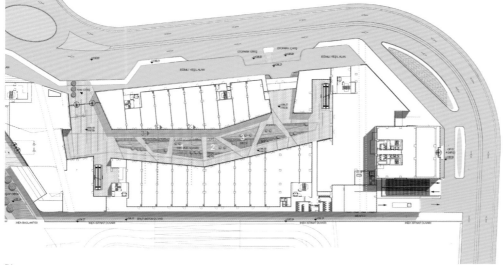

Plan

1. Reflection pool
2. Green area
3. Deck

1. Water and plants combined to offer a comfortable lounge
2. Indoor garden view from upper floor

Manquehue Clinical Centre of Clinica Alemana

The rectangular box made of glass has two holes, shaping two indoor gardens.

Completion date:
2012
Location:
Vitacura, Santiago, Chile
Designer:
MQarquitectos
Photographer:
Nico Saieh
Area:
35,458 sqm

Project Description:

The new Clinical Centre of Clinica Alemana is defined as a modern building. The architecture has simple lines, fine materials, and elements of a sustainable architecture. Its implementation uses high efficiency and the latest technology.

This new medical centre has its main entrance in Avenida Manquehue (eastward), facing the existing façade of the Clínica Alemana Diagnostic Tower. Both buildings achieve consistency since the new design took over the architectural language of the previous building in a contemporary way.

The 6-storey Manquehue Oriente building comprises a 4-storey crystal box on top of a smaller 2-storey structural modular system (also crystal) with this latter providing a very large double height.

The façades of the new building interact in different ways with the outside by forming horizontal brise tiles that are being thick or dense, depending on the sun exposure. To the south, the water garden and in the north side, the land garden.

Around them, the two main areas of the clinic take place, thus, natural light is brought inside, incorporating comfort and allowing significant energy savings.

The Manquehue Oriente building, manages to be functional to the requirements of a worldclass health centre and consolidates its presence in Vitacura-Santiago, covering about 100,000 m².

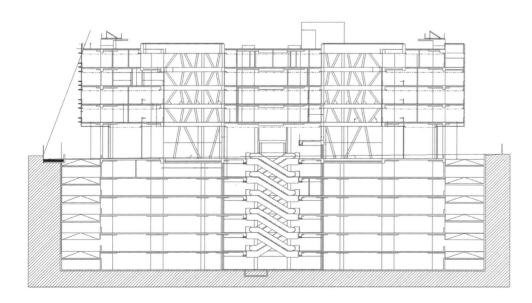

1. A green wall stands behind the reception
2. Water feature below the building
3. Indoor courtyard with water feature

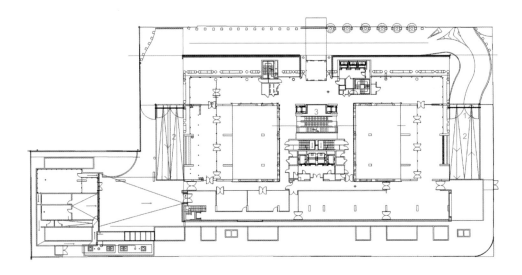

1. Main entrance
2. Indoor garden
3. Stairs

LVM Versicherungen Münster, House 6 + 7

A "Green Strip of Communication", links the different parts of the buildings and leads to the park between the buildings

Completion date:
2010
Location:
Münster, Germany
Designer:
Dipl.-Ing. Gordon Brandenfels
brandenfels
landscape+environment
Photographer:
Andreas Hasenkamp
Area:
35, 700 sqm
Award:
Nordrhein-Westphalia Award
for Architecture, Housing and
Urban Development 2008

Project Description:

The client LVM Versicherungen, a well known insurance company, is constantly expanding. In 2005 an architectual design competition was won for the building 6 and 7 by the Korean architect Duk-Kyu Ryang. Brandenfels landscape + environment was asked by the client to develop an over-all design for the whole site consisting of building 1 to 7.

The landscape design for building 6 and 7 reflects the corporate identity of the LVM Versicherungen: transparency and free, open communication. A "Green Strip of Communication", existing of plants and green epoxy-bound surfaces, links the different parts of the buildings and leads to the park between the buildings. The park, which is close to the canteen, is open for clients, visitors and employees. Large benches invite people to communicate and relax. Three small groves, each consisting of one tree-specie (Liquidamber styraciflua, sweet gum; Ginkgo biloba, ginkgo; Gleditsia triacanthos, gleditsia) are embedded in different planting and lawn areas. The whole park is situated on top of the underground parking.

Inside the building 7 exist two atriums. The

1. Boundary element, 55cm,
with aperture made of V2A steel sheet
2. Artificial stone, 3cm
3. Mortar bed
4. Insulation
5. Bituminous impervious element
plant root safe
6. Protection mat
7. Plant root protective foil
8. Drainage course 8/16 with water retention
9. Filter mat
10. Pond foil, 1.5mm

11. Protection fleece
12. Glass nuggets
13. Connection to base cable
14. Protection mat
15. Plant root protection foil
16. Nomal water level
17. Max. water level
18. Filter mat
19. Combi inspection chat with suction set
20. Alu profile
21. Base 2/32 10cm

office-rooms which are situated along the atriums have a façade with open-able windows. Clean, fresh air is led through
the atrium to the windows. The design of each atrium is supporting this effect by (load reduced) rocks. The rocks mois-
turised by an computer-controled system to force the natural
greening with moss. On the other site of the rocks a water
feature is enriching the air with moisture. Up to 15m high
fishtail-palms (Caryota mitis) create a relaxing atmosphere.
In the courtyard directly connected to the canteen and also
in front of building 6 a large variety of flowering azalea create
a sever contrast to shaped, dark green pine trees.

1. Water feature forms an attraction in the atria
2. Tall fishtail palms grow by the pond
3. View of the internal courtyard garden
4. Courtyard garden

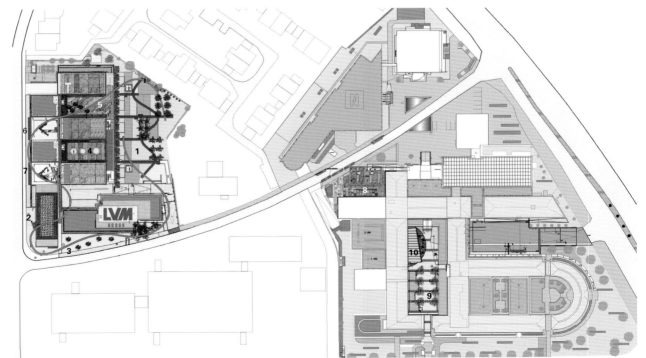

1. Park
2. Entrance
3. Footpath
4. Green roofs
5. Patio
6. Atrium 1
7. Atrium 2
8. Roof cafeteria
9. Patio
10. With smoking pavilion

Singapore Changi Airport Terminal 3

Jungle in the airport

Completion date:
2008
Location:
Singapore
Designer:
CPGairport, CPG Consultants
Pte Ltd
Photographer:
Mr Albert K.S. Lim

Project Description:

Large-scale vertical planting evoking a Southeast Asian equatorial rainforest was introduced into the interior of Singapore's Changi Terminal 3 to structure and soften an otherwise cavernous industrial building. A woven tapestry of living plants not only divides the mega-building in plan into landside/airside sections but also connect the vertical space of the check-in/arrival areas, which are separated by a glass security screen.

Overview

In embarking on its ambitious expansion programme in 2000, Singapore's Changi Airport, perennially named as the best or next-best in the world, intended to raise the bar for excellence in design and to create a monumental iconic first point of entry to the nation-city. Since the landscape design began during the initial stages of project planning the team was able to integrate the building design, the interior design, and the landscape design into a cohesive whole.

Goals

1. To use landscape elements to enhance and to become a dominant feature of the architecture.
2. To develop a unique landscape design palette appropriate to the scale and use of the building.
3. To establish an interior environment where planting is part of the architecture, not just as accents and as decoration.
4. To devise a low-cost, light-weight system for growing massed climbing plants.
5. To confirm the viability of planting in an indoor air-conditioned environment by testing suitable plant species for long-term sustainability.

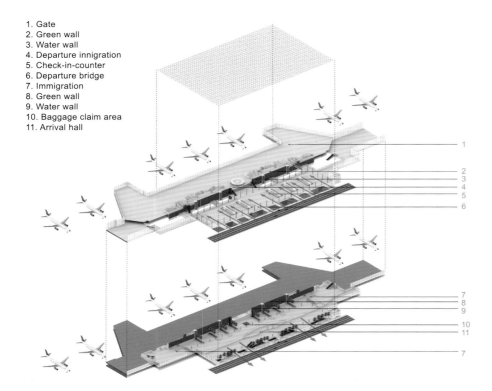

1. Gate
2. Green wall
3. Water wall
4. Departure innigration
5. Check-in-counter
6. Departure bridge
7. Immigration
8. Green wall
9. Water wall
10. Baggage claim area
11. Arrival hall

Site

The site of Changi Airport, one of the busiest hubs in Asia is reclaimed from the sea. The Terminal 3 site, allocated in the airport's initial Master Plan, is on the main axial approach road which terminates at Terminal 1. It is directly across the approach road from Terminal 2, and together the three terminals form a huge cul-de-sac. The interior space is a ten-storey volume, with four functional levels arranged around a huge sky lighted atrium, the base of which is the arrival hall. The roof concept of "butterfly-winged" skylights is a spectacular and dramatic architectural statement, flooding the interior with diffused light, regulated by sensors to control the heat load and ventilation of the immense space. The building is a conservatory for plants.

Programme

1. To treat the most prominent feature of the terminal building - the massive wall which separates the landside check-in arrival hall from the airside departure and shopping lounges.
2. To provide spatial definition and linkage for the vast arrival hall with its eight baggage carousels and omni-directional traffic.
3. To establish a green environment for the interior space, befitting the nation's vision of the arrival to the "City in a Garden".

Master Plan

The landscape Master Plan envisioned the Terminal 3's interior space as a continuation of the overall exterior airport gardens, which are visible through the wide and tall glass "skin" of the building. The green wall is a perfect example of how vertical planting could significantly affect overall interior ambience with a small footprint in plan.

1. The garden looks like a giant green tapestry

Planting Concept

• The granite-clad dividing wall was transformed into a large green wall, a vertical tapestry of climbing and aerial plants. This vertical garden is the building's most distinctive feature, spanning 1000 feet of the 1300 feet length building and at 50 feet high, helped to scale down the high interior space. The structure for the green tapestry is a system of cantilevered I-beams and stainless steel cable structure with planting troughs at every ten feet, covered with vines, creepers and epiphytes. This installation is achieved without sacrificing valuable floor area or compromise to functional requirements.

• The green tapestry exhibits the richness, diversity and character of the Southeast Asian Equatorial Rain Forest. Its bold, dominant form creates a powerful identity for the terminal's vast space.

• A unique characteristic of the tropical rainforest inspired the selection of the more than 10,000 plants for the vertical garden. In the rainforest, vines and epiphytes successfully compete for growing space by lifting themselves off the ground with the help of tall neighbors. In this manner they are able to escape the low light level of the forest floor to reach up to the forest canopy.

• The green tapestry is designed to be maintained easily from catwalks behind the suspended structure. The plants are pre-grown in containers on stainless steel cables which are secured to the structural frame without need of fasteners.

• Perpendicular to the tapestry on the arrival level floor are wide planters with a variety of massed ground covers and majestic Livistona chinensis (Chinese fan-palms).

Water

Four water features 60 feet tall and 20 feet wide made from shredded glass pan-

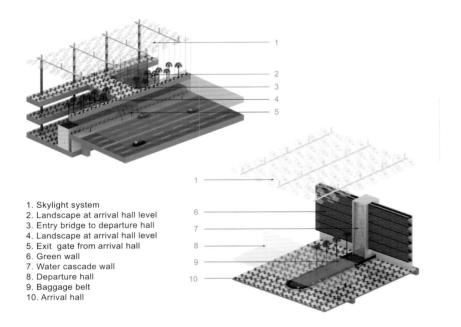

1. Skylight system
2. Landscape at arrival hall level
3. Entry bridge to departure hall
4. Landscape at arrival hall level
5. Exit gate from arrival hall
6. Green wall
7. Water cascade wall
8. Departure hall
9. Baggage belt
10. Arrival hall

els laminated to stainless steel plates, were added to compliment the wall of green. Their shimmering water movement provides texture to create a rhythm of moving light and sparkle against the elegant silence of the green tapestry.

Materials
Tapestry Structure
The planting system is a double-layer cable support system sandwiching fiberglass planting troughs. Stainless steel beams cantilevered from the wall support horizontal I-beam modules with 2 feet wide fiberglass troughs, five segments high. Twining vines on cables in singular containers are easily removed and/or replaced by hand, without mechanical fasteners.

Plant Selection
Plants potentially suitable for the tapestry were installed on test racks in Terminal 1 for four years to ascertain their performance in comparable environmental conditions. Seven species of climbers and a dozen epiphytes were identified as the best candidates, based on growth rate, foliage quality, flowering capability, ease of maintenance and sustainability.

Execution
Design coordination and implementation
The design team of landscape architects/horticulturists/architect, over a period of four years, attended to the project on a regular basis, reviewing hardscape and softscape design, details and performance of the system. Portions of the tapestry were completed while construction was still in progress. The results for plant establishment were initially poor due to constant dust and poor air movement. Plants were imported from neighbouring Malaysia and Thailand and allowed to be acclimated to similar conditions before installation. Pest control was monitored by ensuring that all plant

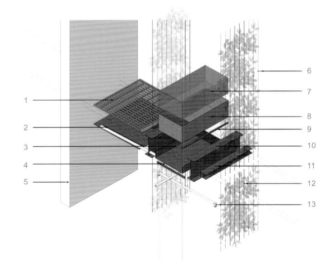

1. Maintenance platform
2. Drainage pipe at 15m inv. PVC(42mm dia) slope to fall connect to outlet
3. 120mm depth gutter laid to fall 1:200 3mm THK stainless steel
4. 30x30 T-bar at 800 interval 3mm THK stainless steel
5. Wall
6. Stainless steel cable
7. Soil mix
8. 480w x3150x1000l gfrc planter
9. Steel spacer
10. L beam
11. 3mm THK grade 306 stainless steel channel to receive cable
12. 1 NOS. climber per cable
13. Fogging nozzles and pipes

specimens brought into the interior was free from infestation. Since natural light is available, the skylights were adjusted to allow maximum light to reach all portions of the green panels. A drip irrigation system is designed to water and fertilise the plant specimens; hand misting is also carried out performing a twofold function: minimizing collection of dust on leaves and foliage feeding. Mock-ups were tested over a period of 4 to 5 years at Terminal 1 which allowed the team to study lighting levels and selection of plant species for optimal performance.

Environmental Concerns
Impact

Terminal 3 is an interior environment subject to stringent controls for human comfort. The plants contribute a visually cooling and refreshing ambience, but do not in any significant way alter the environment of the interior. Pest infestation could become a problem as there is a continuous influx of people and ornamental plants into the terminal. Maintenance is a continuous and long-term issue. The client being sensitive to pest control through non-toxic methods is ensuring that the interior environment is free from noxious and toxic chemicals.

Reinforcement

The green tapestry is not merely a decorative accent but a bold environmental statement complimenting the architecture, demonstrating that landscape as architecture is capable of humanising the interior environment of an enormous and complex building.

Sustainability

As part of an artificial, man-made environment, the Terminal 3 landscape requires continual monitoring. Light (U.V. and infra-red) levels must be sufficient for photosynthesis, and is available from the roof skylights. Humidity is replenished by a misting system and nutrients by drip fertigation. Weak plants are removed and replaced with pre-grown substitutes. The baggage island planters and planting platforms are not individual tree planters, but huge planting troughs with sufficient soil to support long-term life-span of tall palms and shrub groupings.

1. The main body of the vertical garden is a cantilevered system supported by stainless wires
2. Details of the green wall
3. The vertical green wall adds spatial quality to the interior

Red Bull Music Academy

It has the variable relationship between proximity and independence.

Completion date:
2011
Location:
Madrid Spain
Designer:
Langarita-Navarro
Arquitectos, María Langarita
y Víctor Navarro
Photographe:
LUIS DIAZ DIAZ
Area:
4,700 sqm

Project Description:

In many ways this project shares the logic of a Russian matryoshka doll. Not only in the most literal, physical sense, in which one thing is directly incorporated into another, but also in a temporal sense, in which one actually originates within the other. The initial circumstances of this project established a favourable backdrop for this condition:

The Red Bull Music Academy (RBMA) is a nomadic annual music festival. For the last 14 years, this event has been held in a different world city, welcoming the sixty pre-selected international participants and surrounding them with musicians, producers, and DJs, thereby giving them the opportunity to experiment with and exchange knowledge and ideas about the world of music. The 2011 edition of RBMA was going to be held in Tokyo, but given the devastating effects of the earthquake, the location had to be changed. With only five months to plan, the city of

Madrid was selected to hold RBMA.

The RBMA launched the programming for the new Nave de Música (music warehouse), a space specifically dedicated to audio creation and research. Using the existing installation as a starting point and given its experimental character, the construction project was approached as a temporary structure based on the criteria of adaptability and reversibility that would make it easy to completely or partially reconfigure over time.

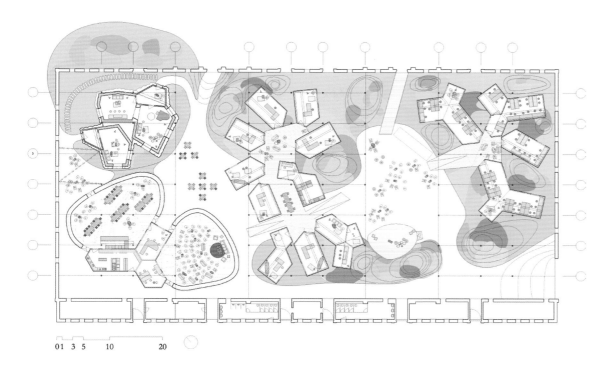

Under these circumstances and in an emergency situation, the work began on an infrastructure capable of meeting the precise technical and acoustic needs of the event, in addition to accelerating, promoting and enriching a series of extremely intense artistic encounters that would take place between the participating musicians, while at the same time adding an environment that would record and archive everything taking place.

The garden is one of the most visible parts of the project of Red Bull Music Academy.

It connects with the memory of the river Manzanares that passes nearby, and of the industry of stockbreeding that the former slaughterhouse formed part of.

It is thought as an Eden that conforms to a common tapestry for all the participants of the academy, functioning as space to hide and to relate.

To achieve this, the species of medium and large size in the garden are planted in flowerpots so that they can be moved to other places after the academy is dismantled. The grouping of these pots gives form to a topography that would be filled with soil in which was the small size species would be planted.

Also, given the temporary nature of this project and in order to avoid influencing future interventions in the warehouse, it was designed to be dismantled in such a way so as to not leave a trace. These criteria gave form to a garden that could have a second life in the future.

As a result, the project unfolded in the warehouse's interior in the form of a fragmented urban structure in which the variable relationship between proximity and independence, and preexistence and performance could offer unexpected stages to its community of inhabitants.

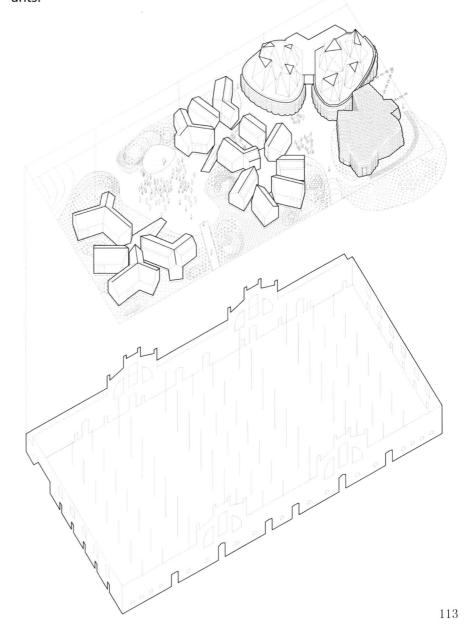

Pfizer Bogota

Full of green plants, the interior design of this new office makes people
feel refreshed and relaxing.

Completion date:
2012
Location:
Bogota, Colombia
Designer:
AEI - Arquitectura e Interiores
Photographer:
Juan Fernando Castro
Area:
6,400 sqm

Project Description:

The new offices of Pfizer in Bogota (Colombia) were a real challenge for Arquitectura e Interiores as it was necessary to adapt the building (built in the 1950s) to the company's new requirements. The designer worked under an open office concept that has a strong emphasis on collaborative spaces such as telephone booths, meeting rooms, informal meeting areas, flexible auditoriums and main cafeteria. It was also necessary to redesign the building's façades and landscaping to modernise it. The design is environmentally-friendly and guarantees employees wellness.

Having gardens inside their offices makes people feel in touch with nature even if they are in a closed space.

The design of Pfizer's offices includes gardens all along the facility, which recreate beautiful natural paths that along with the wood floors, provide a sense of unique tranquility in this corporate space.

This kind of green strategy promotes a better quality of life for offices' occupants, who benefit from these relaxing areas that help them cope with daily stress.

What plants did you choose ?
The plants chosen for the gardens in the Pfizer project are composed of native and/or adapted species that can survive indoors. The plants are ornamental, decorative and of low height. The plants are: Fern, liriope, vinca, rosemary, palms, cartridges and amaranths.

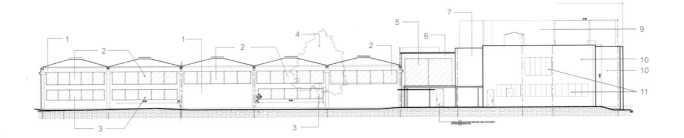

1. Current concrete beams must be painted with WF-7
2. Current glazing's frame must be painted with aluminum gray color.
3. New 10mm tempered glazing in alumina system or similar
4. The current tree must be kept
5. The tempered glass façade's frame could be painted if necessary
6. Current masonry Wall with WF-7 finish
7. Facade plane must be painted with WF-7
8. New 10mm tempered glass door, see door schedule in A-10.0 sheet
9. All exterior walls in the machine room must be stuccoed and painted with wf7
10. Facade plane with superboard covering and wf7 finish
11. Current glazing

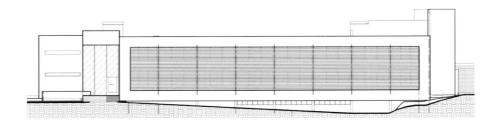

How to water the plants ?How to maintain the plants ?
Due to their characteristics, the plants require little watering and maintenance can be performed by the office's cleaning staff.
Initially, when they were seeded it was necessary to water the plants daily with enough water to ensure their recovery after planting them. Once the plants were adapted to the environment, irrigation was every third day.

How to air the room when plants send out CO_2 ?
Also, Pfizer offices have an exhaust ventilation system that evacuates CO_2 produced inside and circulates fresh air to meet air quality requirements.

1. Thriving Spathiphyllum kochii in the lounge area

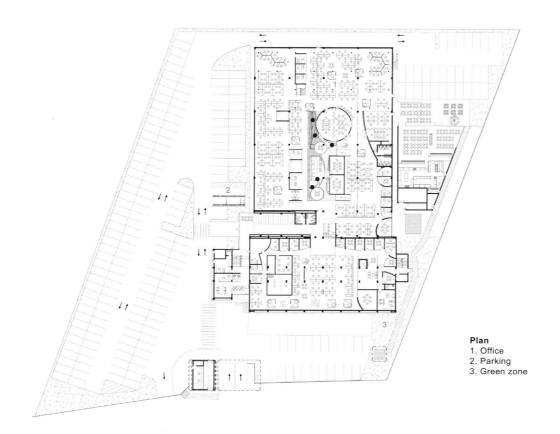

Plan
1. Office
2. Parking
3. Green zone

1. Vertical garden in the hallway
2. Plants outside the office area
3. Indoor garden with multiple layers
4. Office area

Alexander Forbes Headquarters

The visitor and the employee are able to experience diversity throughout the work days without the monotony of conventional work spaces.

Completion date:
2013
Location:
Johannesburg,South Africa
Designer:
Paragon
Landscape designer:
Karen James
Photographer:
Andrew Bell
Area:
100,000 sqm (construction area)
37,500 sqm (rentable area)

Project Description:

The tenant areas of Alexander Forbes at 115 West Street can be divided into four spatial types:
· the client interface spaces
· the open plan floor plates
· the common break-out facilities or pause areas
· the executive level

The function and tone of each of these spatial types served to interpret and formulate the design brief. The client interface areas were required to be elegant and refined, while at the same time they had to be personable and needed to accommodate the wide range of Alexander Forbes clients from investor to individual. Paragon Interface interpreted these requirements with a range of textures that were tactile and warm with a connection to nature.

Upon arrival in the main atrium, the visitor encounters two noticeable asymmetrical reception pods. These ribbed structures are designed to shade the reception staff from the moving path of the sun, penetrating the skylight cones eight floors above. Modelled by Revit software, the pods assume an intriguing organic form of their own. They are clad in bamboo to add an immediate feeling of warmth as the user enters this light filled volume.

The rugs and the carpets in the client interface areas were modelled from rock strata while again a bamboo veneer was used to clad the wall surfaces. This softens the multiple-volumed glazed atria while ficus benjamina punctuate the atrium voids and over time will envelop the lower bridges, generating a forest walk sensation. The tables in the

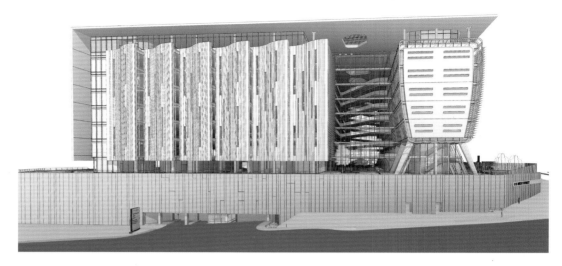

Elevation 1

meeting suites continue the soft play with organic forms complementing the irregular plans of the base build service elements positioned at the centre of each client interface suite.

The finishes of the tenanted areas work together with those found in the base build areas to create a workplace environment that is cordial and open to visitors as well as employees.

Elevation 2

The floor plates reflect the desire of Alexander Forbes that office's structures remain non-hierarchical and finishes more utilitarian in nature. A desire for collaborative teamwork and open communication among staff, led to the creation of large open plan floor plates with bench style cluster work stations. These are interspersed with some open door cubicles and a few offices for executives only.

The furniture and finishes in these areas is more neutral with a reduced palette of textures. Simple painted and wall papered surfaces adjoin a single overall carpet colour, with inlays that demarcate circulation routes only. The workstations and ancillary furniture are all white with black upholstered elements.

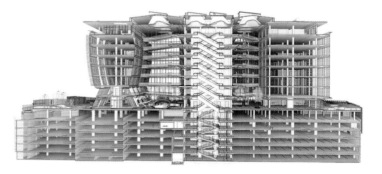

Section

In contrast to the restrained floor plates, the pause areas on each floor have a far more playful character. They are designed to stimulate and encourage creativity. The pause areas are saturated with colour that can be experienced throughout the multiple volumes of the north atrium. They are ornamented with moulded bamboo walls which appear to be continuously moving as well as magnetic walls on

which an array of games, including scrabble and fridge poetry can be played.

The tone of the executive level reflects the richness and layering of experience that the company seeks to communicate with its clients. Art gathered over time, articulates the warm spaces which flow between the volumes that lead Alexander Forbes.

As a whole the collective experience of the spatial types employed at Alexander Forbes provides a varied and active work environment. Where the visitor and the employee are able to experience diversity throughout the work day without the monotony of conventional work spaces.

For landscaping and planting on the ground floor north and south, xeriscaping made use of indigenous plants throughout, except the Ficus Benjamina in the atriums. Planter walls are constructed from off shutter concrete, which create pockets of meeting areas. The building has been accredited with a 4 Star Green Star Design V1 rating.

1. Interior water feature
2. Colorful furniture of main waiting area

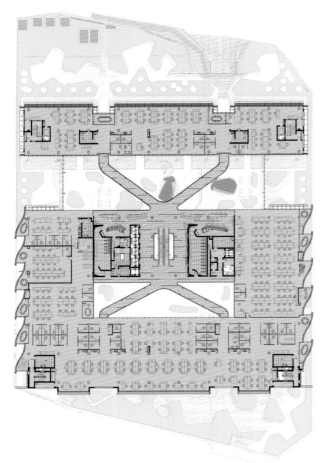

Typical plan of an office floor

1. Ficus are also to be found in the indoor multifunctional area
2. Lounge area
3. Staff dining area
4. Vibrantly coloured lounge area
5. Washroom

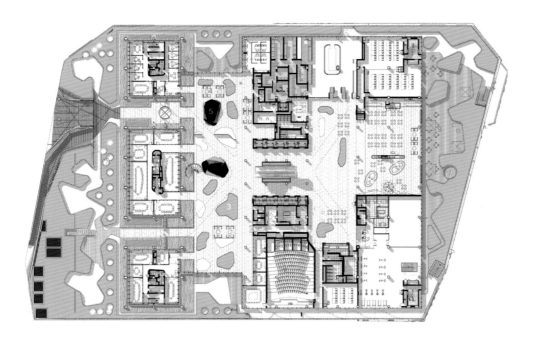

Ground Floor Plan
1. Staff indoor restaurant
2. Water pond
3. Ficus Benjamina trees with light
4. Rest area
5. Reception
6. Stairs
7. Auditorium
8. Washroom
9. Outside rest area & staff outside restaurant

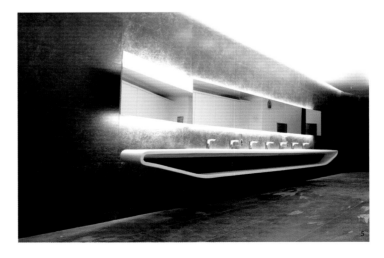

Orona Hernani

The idea was to create an exuberant indoor space with palm trees and a pond.

Completion date:
2008
Location:
Hernani, Spain
Designer:
LUR PAISAJISTAK S.L.
Photographer:
LUR PAISAJISTAK S.L.
Area:
1,420 sqm

Project Description:

Orona is a company that builds lifts internationally and belongs to the world's biggest cooperative (Grupo Mondragon). Located in Hernani, the factory made a modernisation process and the offices grew creating an indoor space for workers and visitors.

Orona's activity centres on the design, manufacturing, installation, maintenance and modernization of mobility solutions, such as lifts, escalators and moving walkways. All key to integral service.

Leading group in the European markets, and which enjoys international prestige. Orona develops mobility solutions: lifts, escalators and moving walkways.

Behind a brand lies a business culture. The business culture of Orona is characterised by the following three values: commitment, reliability and agility.

The idea was to create an exuberant indoor space with palm trees and a pond. The arrangement of the planters and the pond was done locating rectangles through the indoor space. The planters periphery was designed wide enough to enable the workers to sit at them while having a break.

The selected palm tree is the Arecastrum romanzofianum, which has developed a very good growth in these indoor conditions.

The pond acts as an eye-catching feature to visitors and brings freshness and water sound to this indoor space.

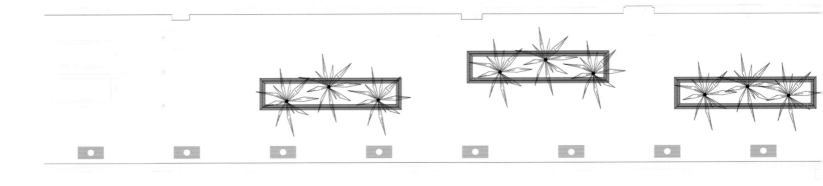

1. Palm trees
2. Pond

1. Wooden chairs are placed beside plant containers

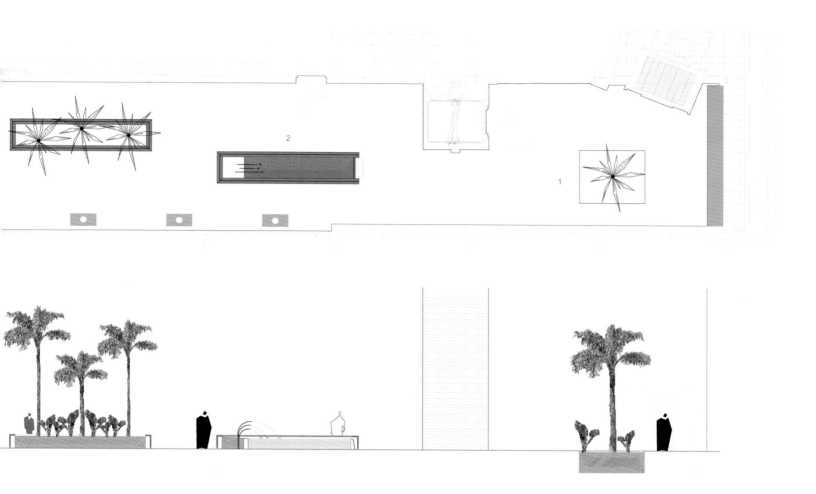

Residential Centre Cugat Natura

An interior garden is visible from almost every corner of the big room, improving the environment of the users through an appropriate level of brightness and optimal comfort.

Completion date:
2012
Location:
Barcelona, Spain
Designer:
JFARQUITECTES
Photographer:
Xavi Gálvez
Area:
17,900 sqm

Project Description:

The Residential Cugat Natura Centre is located in one of the most peaceful and exclusive zones of the city of Sant Cugat del Vallès (Barcelona), enjoying one of the most privileged views of the Golf Club of the locality and a directly access to the city centre.

One important aspect of this kind of project is trying to understand which kind of users will use this center, and the needs that they have. In this residential centre we can clearly differentiate between two different users; on one hand, those who haven't got any degree of dependence, and that would like to have in their common lives the facilities that a residential center offers them, and on the other hand, people with a low-medium-high degree of dependence who need to be looked after and handled by professionals.

Under those premises as a crux of the project, a residential centre made up of two building has been designed. Both buildings have a ground floor plus three floors more, linked between them by the two basements. The first volume is earmarked as a geriatric residential, for users with some degree of dependence, and the other volume, further away, are assisted apartments with access to all the services of the centre.

A residential centre is required to provide a quality of life equal to or better than what their users used to have before entering. It has to be a pleasant place to live, coexist and also to visit, and create encouraging sensations to the people that are probably going to spend the last days of their lives there.

To make this possible, the residential centre not only has a build surface around 17,000 m^2 for rooms, services and polyvalent rooms, it is also surrounded by about almost 4,000 m^2 of green exterior zones for taking a walk and do activities with the staff from the center.

Geriatric building

The building is understood as two big volumes, constructer from ceramic brick, and a central core, built with reinforced concrete and curtain wall, which contains the main vertical movements of the building. It has 86 double rooms, placed on the three-storey and releasing space in some

1. Exterior view of the apartment
2. Indoor garden

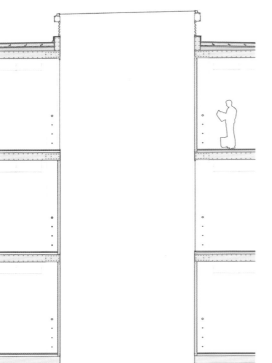

1. Pladur 15+15+70+15+15+white vescom facing
2. Tubular subestructure supporting the carpentry of the glass
3. Invert u steel galvanise profile supporting the glass
4. Continuous celling of pladur 15+45
5. Registrable celling arsmstrong 60x60 cm
6. Double glass
7. U steel galvanise profile supporting the glass,white finishing
8. Brick wall
9. Wall facing plastered and painted in white
10. Gradient formation
11. Waterproofing
12. Gardening soil

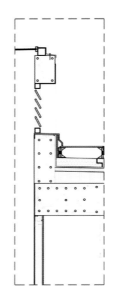

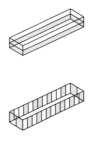

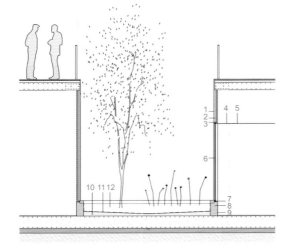

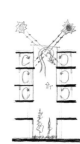

2

1. Hall
2. Indoor garden view from the third floor
3. Interior garden view from the basement 1 corridor
4. Details of the indoor garden

zones of the floors for achieve the answer to the need of create diverse rest points or polyvalent rooms. The ground floor of the building contains the public program, reception, administration, polyvalent room, café, dining hall, physiotherapy room, and zones for resting.

To avoid giving the impression of a hospital, with endless long corridors and doors into both sides, two big atriums in the rooms zone and another smaller on the hall were projected, allowing and providing the entry of natural light to all room floors and lower floors, even to the basement -1 with a large interior garden.

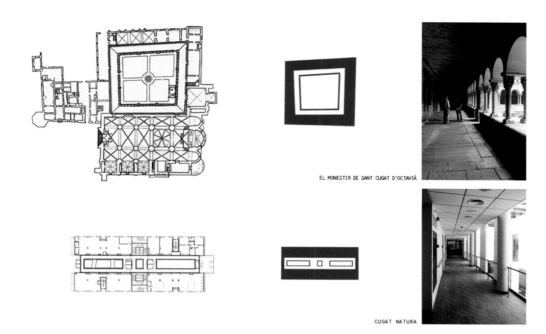

EL MONESTIR DE SANT CUGAT D'OCTAVIÀ

CUGAT NATURA

Apartment Building

The apartment building, materialised too, respecting the buildings around it, made with ceramic brick, and concrete walls on the extremes, was designed following a staircase-shaped system for the floors. With this measure it can be achieved that all the 32 apartments can enjoy of one open and private terrace with views to the Golf club. The apartments have all the equipment necessary to move in and there are two typologies, with 55 m^2 and 46 m^2 net. In these, the interior designers, have enhanced the width sensation through the distribution, the use of natural light, the lighting, and the use of the materials in coatings. The lobbies and corridors work as a common nexus between the apartments and the polyvalent room through the language and constructive solutions used in both areas.

Underground Floor – Linkage

On the basement -1, were both buildings merge, there are three different programme areas. There is an interior garden (with vegetal plantation) on this floor and it is visible from almost every corner of the big room, improving the environment of the users through an appropriate level of brightness and optimal comfort.

Chapter Five

Landscape Design of Commercial Interior

5.1 Indoor Garden Helps to Increase Sales

Retailers have long understood the importance of store environment in enhancing the shopping experience. The outdoor landscape can be a seamless extension of shop interiors, providing indoor/outdoor continuity for a positive shopping experience. Urban forestry can play an important role in business districts. Interior plants and landscape may create store interiors more favorable for retail activity.

Through the medium of plants the centre successfully translates outside to inside and relaxes almost everybody, all ages and types of people re-lated to the atmosphere. The result for the public is a perfect environment for the purposes of shopping and leisure. Fig.5.1 and 5.2

Fig.5.1 and 5.2 Collapsible Leaves, 2013, Isetan Shinjuku, designed by Azuma Makoto. Azuma was glad to receive many admiring comments on their creation. The customers said that they were overwhelmed by the impact of the entrance decoration, the plants are mainly, cast-iron planet, danae, liriope, dracaena and black leaf, and they created many different patterns by folding them in various ways.

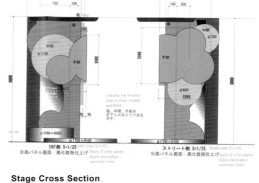

Stage Cross Section

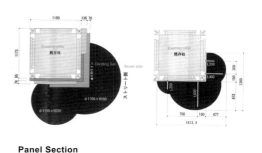

Panel Section

Commercial interior planning must be practical in addition to pretty. It should provide an appropriate atmosphere for clients and employees. The previous should wish to return and also the latter should wish to enter into work each morning.

The look of commercial interior landscape must produce a warm space that's inviting and soothing to site visitors and comfy and simple to employees. Site visitors should have the ability to sit inside a comfortable waiting area that's fitted with appropriate commercial furniture and optimum lighting. The atmosphere ought to be cheerful, not dour.

5.2 Landscape Features of Typical Commercial Interiors

5.2.1 Indoor landscape of restaurants

Interior landscaping can make a significant contribution to the decor and theme of a restaurant, and it can lend a warm, relaxing ambience conducive to comfortable dining. Even fast-food chains have recognised the importance of enhancing their establishments to accommodate a broader portion of the working class that might otherwise brown-bag it each day. To cater to that clientele, they have expanded seating, experimented with fashionable colours for the walls, put up paintings, and, of course, landscaped their interiors. Fig.5.3

Fig.5.3 Japonez CDA, designed by Guillermo Arredondo,, the restaurant bringing nature into the interior design, to create different environments that would evoke emotions and diverse experiences in the restaurant. A green module wall of hanging plant pots and drip irrigation system is of simple construction and convenient for interiors. Considering the location of the restaurant and climate of Mexico City, local plants were selected to easily withstand the environment and minimize the maintenance. The textures of the plants soften the rigidity of the other walls creating contrast and style.

Preliminary planning

Successful interior landscaping in restaurants requires careful preliminary planning to overcome the various technical problems that can occur as a result of inherent environmental factors. Low light, air conditioning, difficult access and customer traffic are only a few of the nuisances that interior landscapers must anticipate during the design process.

Becoming involved in the initial planning stages with the architect or designer can help minimise the severity of some of these problems. Determining the correct lighting and plant placements early on can contribute significantly to the success of the final design, as well as the interior landscape's longevity.

Restaurant themes and styles

Every restaurant has its own distinct theme or style, be it French haute cuisine, Mexican, Italian, casual (such as hamburgers or pizza), lobster bar or steak house. Only after the interior landscaper has examined the style can a suitable design be created.

For example, Mexican restaurants, a favourite in southern California, are characteristically furnished with tile walls, natural woods, water features, occasional antiques and, in the less formal establishments, old signs and bric-a-brac reminiscent of California's early days under Spanish rule. Fig.5.4

Fig.5.4 D'amico 1 de 4, designed by CHEREMSERRANO. The whole atmosphere, complemented with light, water and green areas, will surround the costomers and evolve while enjoying the chef's specialties.

Interior landscapes in such establishments usually consist of hanging and cascading plants and a few free-standing tall shrubs or trees. Colourful chrysanthemums and kalanchoes are sometimes added for accent. There is seldom any rhyme or reason to the plant selection; it's usually as random as the decor's other elements. The emphasis is on filling every empty space and creating an overgrown garden atmosphere.

The interior of an Italian restaurant may look quite different. It's a more sparsely decorated space with low light levels, less foliage and, in some of the more elegant establishments, an emphasis on cut flower arrangements.

On the other hand, high-tech style coffeehouses offer even few plants. They're typically characterised by bare-brick or stucco walls, hardwood floors, and wide-open spaces highlighted by only the faintest hint of foliage.

The look in fast-food and family restaurants is distinctly cozy and home-like. These are places you can take the kids and watch them scale the walls while you try to eat and have a conversation at the same time. The atmosphere is definitely less formal, with a much higher concentration of plants than most other eateries. Fig.5.5

Fig.5.5 McDonalds, the landscape design introduces nature and leisure into the dining area.

Designing interior landscapes for restaurants sounds pretty simple so far. However, in reality, each design required more than just selecting plants to complement the existing decor; someone had to make some practical decisions about what would actually survive there. The problems that exist in restaurants have forced many interior landscapers to say "no" when asked for estimates.

Technical problems

Besides the financial risks involved in interior landscaping a restaurant, technical problems abound. As in any commercial space, interior landscapers must be concerned about the environmental factors of lighting, air circulation and temperature. However, in a restaurant, there are additional problems with grease, dust, nicotine, drafts, and smog. Finally, there are also problems of limited access time for maintenance, abuse by patrons and staff, and limitations for insect control.

All these details must be taken into consideration during the design process. If an interior landscape cannot hold up to the maintenance, it probably has a poor design. However, for restaurants, it is extremely difficult to design anything that is maintainable, unless you really put your mind to finding the right solutions to the problems that limit the designs and could cause heavy plant losses.

Find a plant that is easy to care for and grows in a closet, and you have the ideal restaurant plant. Find one that doesn't shed leaves on the customers' heads and food, tables, chairs, window sills and floors, and you've got the best plant ever for restaurants.

Now find a plant that does not suffer from regular infestations by mites or related pests and requires little moisture to survive, and you have found the answer to an interior landscaper's dream. Fig.5.6 and 5.7

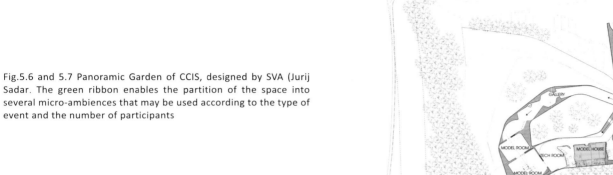

Fig.5.6 and 5.7 Panoramic Garden of CCIS, designed by SVA (Jurij Sadar. The green ribbon enables the partition of the space into several micro-ambiences that may be used according to the type of event and the number of participants

Flowering plants

Last, but not least, are exotic flowering plants which can contribute greatly to original and stunning dining atmospheres. Orchids, bromeliads, and other epiphytic plants are often used to enhance what would otherwise be ordinary interior landscapes.

In addition, bromeliads and Tillandsia come in many shapes and sizes, some of which do better under different lighting or temperature regimes. There are plenty of experts who can advise the novice on their selection and maintenance. Despite the problems mentioned above, restaurant interior landscapes offer may possibilities for creativity. It might even be argued that imagination is the primary limitation in achieving spectacular results.

5.2.2 Indoor landscape of retails
Interior landscaping can brighten up retail

Shops and the lovely goods they contain are obviously the biggest attractions when people visit the mall, but customers are spending longer than ever before in shopping centers due to the range of goods and services on offer (Fig.5.8). There are, however, several other factors that contribute to a more enjoyable shopping experience. When the shopping malls are considered as public buildings, interior landscaping can also reflect the identity or culture of that specific community where the shopping malls are constructed. Mainly, three types of landscaping are used in interior volumes. They are live, dried or artificial landscaping. Depending on building characteristics, size, and expectations from interior volumes, the types of plants selected and their arrangements are changed. While small size plants in pots preferred for residential buildings big trees/plants are used for public buildings like shopping malls and offices that have bigger volumes. On the other hand, if there is no natural light in an interior volume, generally live plants will dry. Therefore, artificial plants are preferred in this type of spaces.

Comfortable enough to spend

Malls are almost always completely enclosed in a temperature controlled environment. Glass ceilings provide natural light to make the mall feel bright and spacious, and customers can take shelter from bad weather

Fig.5.8 This installation for renewal opening is by far the biggest scale among past installations Azuma Makoto has done at Isetan department store. Isetan department store's requirement was, "decorate a building with uniqueness, something outstanding and which matches Isetan's special grand renewal opening occasion rather than just an aggregate of massive flowers." Then, Azuma suggested a leaf installation, which could overrule a concept of "celebration=flower", like a composition where leaves eroding the store. Since plants are living, they naturally dry out. The team members were there everyday for 3 weeks for maintenance, thus they managed to show all process by which leaves slowly decay and/or transform, as a part of the installation. He thinks it was one of the new approaches to show botanical work.

and noisy traffic. Tastefully selected music can add a sense of tranquillity to the space, whilst large pavilions ensure that customers do not feel cramped. The other hugely important aspect of this complete experience is the use of plants or natural features to enhance the appearance of the mall. This process is known as interior landscaping, and there are some very successful demonstrations of this in malls across the world.

5.2.3 Indoor landscaping and green plants in the hotel industry

Throughout hotels in Europe and Asia, and especially in countries like Holland and Japan, indoor landscaping is as common as tulips and chopsticks, because the cultural and social relevance is embedded in their way of life. However, some hotel brands in the United States have made plant life and interior landscaping a top priority since their inception and even incorporated the practice into their brand standards. Fig.5.9 and 5.10 Some hotel requires that 50 percent of each hotel atrium be covered in live plants and water elements, such as waterfalls and streams, and 20 percent of the decorative railings overlooking the atrium must incorporate living plant life. Although interior landscaping adds another significant

Fig.5.9 Quality Hotel Expo, designed by Haptic Architects Ltd. Subtle lighting has been installed to work with the planted trees, where shadows from their canopies dance upon the articulated lobby ceiling.

Fig.5.10 The lounge has an overall wilder look with some large leaved plants like Fatsia, Elettaria and Anthurium, together with colourful begonias setting the main character of the wall. A few varieties of Nephrolepis ferns add to the typically lush character of this kind of undervegetation.

element to hotel operations, the practice adds irreplaceable value for the guests and makes the working environment much more pleasant for the hotel staff. Hotel guests experience atriums differently, depending on the nature of their stay.

Although some hoteliers balk when they hear that a team of 20 full-time horticulturists maintains Opryland's luxurious greens, such extensive landscaping isn't necessary to obtain the benefits that come with interior plant life. Many times hotels don't see the benefit of indoor landscaping inside the venue as well as outside because of the cost and labor associated with the practice. But before they rule it out they need to find out what green plants can live in that environment and don't require as much maintenance.

Determining which indoor house plants would bring about the most benefits within a given space is difficult for hoteliers to do on their own, unless they have the time for the research. Although the cost varies from one hotel to another, interior landscaping really doesn't impact the overall per-key costs. The greenery has a calming effect on the guests and team members alike. From a guest standpoint, many arrive and start taking photos of the lobby atrium.

Plants at Work spends the bulk of its financing on crunching data and disseminating information, without a doubt that plants add value to employees' working environments, and productiveness, and therefore improves guests' experiences in hotels.

Hotels can also keep guests in the lobby, gift shop, and atrium longer when the interior landscaping has a nature element. Guest use of the atrium area or the snack bar increases almost four percent in hotels. The studies also demonstrated a drop in anxiety among both men and women when plants, water, and light were in the vicinity.

Tanishq Store

The design of the store brings these two together in a "garden," an oasis where the customer is free to relax while her senses are enlivened by the depth of the experience.

Completion date:
2008
Location:
Chicago, USA
Designer:
Pompei A.D.
Photographer:
Randhir Singh
Area:
177 sqm

Project Description:

The concept for the Tanishq store developed out of a study of the relationship between customer and jewelry, along with the role that nature plays in binding them together. Jewelry is created by taking elements from nature and refining them. Human beings are similar in that we are products of nature but have spent our lives refining ourselves. The design of the store brings these two together in a "garden," an oasis where the customer is free to relax while her senses are enlivened by the depth of the experience.

Customers are initially drawn to the store by the sculptural storefront. From a distance, views into the store are diffused by a delicate laser cut screen. A large canopy extends overhead, drawing people to take a closer look at

the display boxes suspended in the screen. From here, the customer is able to peek through the screen into the store, creating a sense of excitement.

An organic non-orthogonal layout inside the store encourages customers to meander through the space. With multiple pathways, the customer creates her own unique experience as she walks around sculptural elements displaying jewelry. Plants cascade over the tops of white concrete and terra-cotta coloured plaster walls, culminating in a wall of ivy across the back of the store.

By rethinking the entire jewelry buying experience, the store design creates opportunities for better interaction between the employees

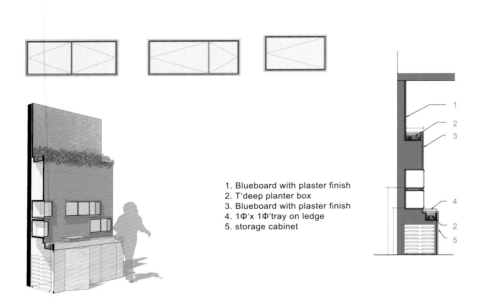

1. Blueboard with plaster finish
2. 1' deep planter box
3. Blueboard with plaster finish
4. 1Φ'x 1Φ' tray on ledge
5. storage cabinet

and customers. As customers walk along the wall mounted jewelry display niches, the store employees are able to stand next to them and talk to them about the jewelry. Additionally, there are 5 tables and a lounge spread around the store encouraging customers to sit and relax while shopping.

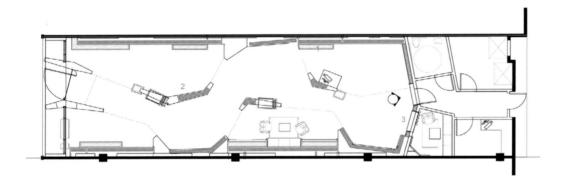

1. High wall with pothos
2. Lower wall with moss
3. Living wall with pothos

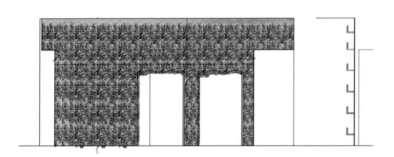

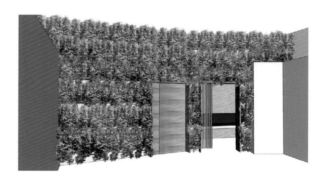

1. Interior view with display cases, wall cases, and growing moss
2. Sales table, recess tiered wall displays and plantings

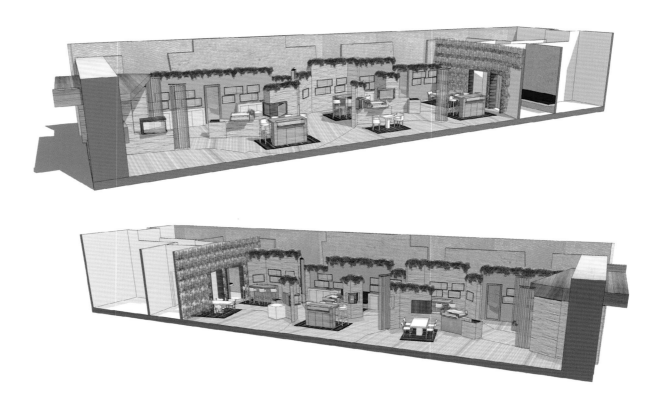

HARE

In order to create a relaxed atmosphere where people could stay longer taking items to items in hand, Hare is designed with extreme care to be taken that it's "not obviously designed".

Completion date:
2012
Location:
Fukuoka, Japan
Designer:
Takashi Mitsuhashi, Takuya Hirayama, PEBBLE Co., Ltd.
Photographer:
Kozo Takayama
Area:
200 sqm
Main Materials:
wood, steel, mortar, plaster, paint, mirror, etc.

Project Description:

"HARE" is a fashion brand for both sexes, offering "basic line" and "own style" with the concept of "to be the part of life". By the request of the brand director, the store was designed quite simple by cutting off decorations as much as possible, yet remaining the principle and peculiar taste of the brand casually into its interior.

Men's area is coordinated in monotone based colors such as black, white and gray. On the other hand, women's area is differentiated by adding gentle wooden materials and champagne gold in white based interior.

The patio-like area in the center of the store with a ceiling light which resembles sunshine was designed to provide a comfortable space for customers, especially for couples, to feel free to sit and chat in the store while selecting items.

Some of the plants in the façade were originally planted in the middle of the store. To get the most of it, PEBBLE enhanced the green area by adding ivy over the wall and under the original plants. People in the store will be put under the illusion that they are standing out in the open air even though they are in the store.

The concrete finish wall obliquely sticking out on the right upper side of the store breaks the monotony and gives move to the wall behind the hanger pipe. This unique design leads people to lift their eyes and walk further into the store spontaneously without stopping or going back. The wall in the left front side of the store where two mannequins are standing is also obliquely cut to lead people smoothly into the ladies booth.

1. Planting
2. Flowerbed fixtures
3. Matte urethane paint finish woodwork
4. Bench unit
5. Flowerbed fixtures

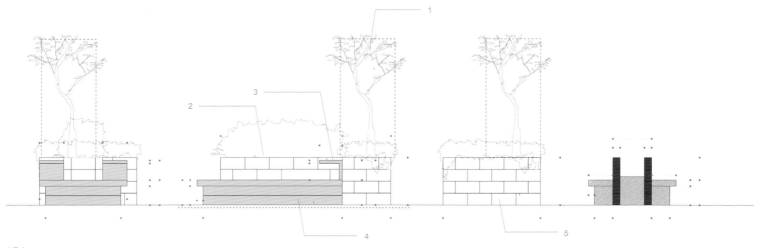

1. Comfortable seating near the plants provides resting area for the customers

2. Seen from the side, the interior landscape consists of three levels of plant, seating and gravel

3-4. The clothing section for women uses a white colour scheme with a tint of wood and champagne while the section for men adopts the three colours of black, white and grey

Rise Hair Brand miino

Beauty salon based on the concept a "resort".

Completion date:
2012
Location:
osaka,japan
Designer:
ryo isobe (r.isobe+office for design)
Area:
168 sqm

Project Description:

Not to be found anywhere, the only concept of the beauty salon here is a "resort". The earl wall diagonal is loaded with Ryukyu stone. The slit of a tree light makes shadows. The cave-like shampoo booth is accompanied with a water Garden to illuminate the fluctuation. The entrance Garden is also covered in planting.

All the elements produce a resort feeling by setting to contrast the modern elements, such as shelves curved lighting and the hanging huge stainless steel mirror finish, creating a modern space that is not too far to the Oriental.

In contrast with the elements that produce a sense of resort, the designers aim to create an oriental and modern space, such as masonry walls made in the shape of the Ryukyu areas' garden, leading to the store from the outside and the modern element. You can also see the curved wooden shelves and floating stainless objects. Planting of tropical external is connected to the waiting area in the store.

Ring made of stainless steel polished has been suspended around the salon. It functions as an accent of the space, and also highlights the curve of the wall of the Ryukyu masonry. The entire nail booth is covered with a wooden slit area, like a simple canopy for each seat in there. In addition, thin sliced curtain was suspended in the opening facing the outside of the booth. Instead of texture of these elements, it was the subject of the configuration space how light and shadows work when it was illuminated by lighting.

1. WC
2. Vip booth
3. Nail booth
4. Cut booth
5. Water garden
6. Shampoo booth
7. Stock
8. Colour booth
9. Shopping booth
10. Terrace
11. Garden

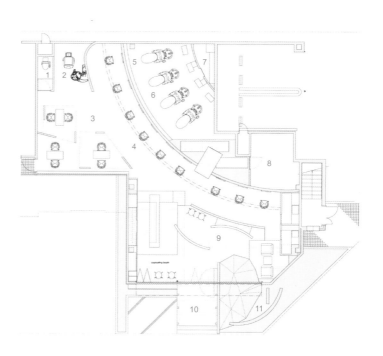

1. Waiting booth & inner garden
2. Waiting booth
3. VIP booth & Bamboo arranged in a random
4. Nail booth
5. Cut booth & floating curved mirrored SUS lighting object & ryukyu stone wall

Blub Lounge Club

One of the crucial areas for more sophisticated clients, the VIP area, is designed with vertical rows of different plant species, dividing the space into geometric modules of varying heights to create a natural, living environment which both protects and provides privacy for those who want to get away from the crowds.

Completion date:
2010
Location:
Barcelona, Spain
Designer:
Elia Felices Interiorismo
Photographer:
Rafael Vargas
Area:
600 sqm

Project Description:

The club is a space with capacity to combine evening dining with music and a discotheque.

The lighting, shapes, colours, furniture and the space itself create the experience of forming part of an undersea world. The light shining onto the different elements is broken up into tiny shafts, resembling the rays of light under the sea, bathing every detail in an underwater glimmer.

Blub lounge is a small sub-aquatic world. The first immersion takes place as people come through the door with its vegetable, organic imagery.

The open interior space enables circuits of interaction to be established. Movement between the different public areas has been made easier by the use of divisions built into the walls, using new elements such as the blue anodised aluminium Kriska® curtains, which link up to make a light and versatile mesh screen on the upper part of the walls which is both decorative and functional in that it allows spaces to be defined while providing light, colour and movement similar to that of water.

The space has been organized to operate on one practically rectangular level, where the various areas are marked by differences in height. Among the curves on the left side,

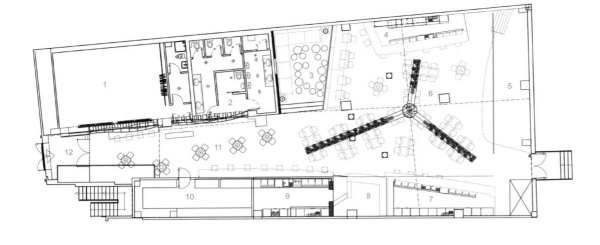

1:150

0m 1m 2m 3m

people find their first companion, a mermaid, formed by a collage of plates, coloured glass and bottle openers. A long vertical mirror in the wall at the entrance expands the space and reflects the diversity of the place. From there we move into the central restaurant area, where the tables are aligned and distributed around a metal Y-shaped structure, creating several geometric patterns and ambiences as required by the occasion. It can then be transformed into a dance floor.

Two symmetrical bars reinforce the concept by having a decoration based on semi-circular shapes, a green-blue colour scheme and more vegetation. They are topped by ECO Starlight by Cosentino, making curved black surfaces made of recycled materials, which provide a shimmer that is appropriate for the setting while making use of a product that is innovative, ecological and sustainable through its manufacturing process and composition. Similarly, the rear wall of the bar is decorated with a chic palm tree made of a collage of coloured glass to go with the bottles on either side of it.

The stage, rising like rock from the seabed, gives a complete view of the premises. The coloured RGB LED lighting and lamps like trailing seaweed that intertwine with the beams of light are a fundamental part of this microcosm. The banks of theatrical spotlights add to the unique and sophisticated character of the place. The furniture has been exclusively designed to blend into the architectural setting. The layout makes the space suitable for a number of uses; concerts, discotheque, restaurant, VIP area and drinks lounge. The space has been designed to be flexible and versatile so that a wide range of activities can be held here.

1. The vibrant LED lighting are like trailing seaweed, shining above the dining tables.
2. Green and blue colour scheme and plant decoration are adopted at the bar
3. The bar is finished with a black curve of recycled material, soaked in a melody of light

D'Amico

The stones provoke a changing texture where not only light and shadow emerge from their surface, but also were natural vegetation grow and change with time.

Completion date:
2011
Location:
Bosques de las Lomas, Mexico
Designer:
CHEREMSERRANO
Photographer:
Jaime Navarro

Project Description:

D'Amico, "between friends", is an Italian restaurant of family tradition in which the love of cooking and passing on recipes come from many generations back. For the clients, to think of gastronomy is "to immerse themselves into endless stories and anecdotes were each recipe becomes an experience and devotion, leaving only the essence and unique flavor of their inherited dishes". The owner wanted to create a striking environment that would enhance their high quality food, offering a warm personalised experience.

The design premise was to create a living space where natural materials would surround the surfaces provoking a detachment of the noisy city – a restaurant where people could come with their couple or families and enjoy a nice dinner resulting on a changing experience. The chosen materials were natural stones brought from Puebla that were placed in the walls and light wood in the floor. The wood has a look of old plank which very nicely contrasts with the dark stones. The whole atmosphere, complemented with light, water and green areas, will surround the costomers and evolve while enjoying the chef's specialties.

The restaurant is distributed into two levels. In the lower level you can find the main public area, divided into different scenarios: a wine tasting bar with high tables located next to the entrance, the main dining area with double height, and the outdoor-smoking terrace contained in a glass box of single height. Behind a green wall made out of stones, is located the kitchen with high technology equipment, according to the client and chefs requirements.

The hustle of the kitchen is buffered from the serenity of the dining area, but easily accessed. The bar in the dining area hides the stair that brings you up to the public restrooms, which are located in the upper level. Also in the upper level, connected by a service entrance and the lower kitchen, you can find the required private services and administrative offices. The furniture in the public areas was exclusively designed for D'Amico, in collaboration with Paul Roco.

In order to hide a central column and provide a space for possible projection of videos, a black glass chimney was designed in the dining area, which provokes a game of reflections enlarging the space. Green planters were added into some walls, as well as trees and palms to separate the main façade from the street. The ceiling is painted in black and by separating the perimeter from the walls, the light enters provoking a sense of continuity to the stone walls. The whole atmosphere provides an impression of light and dramatic context full with textures, light and shadows, in which the food becomes the natural focus of attention.

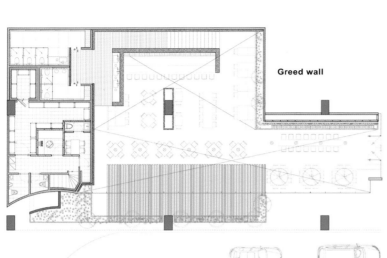

Greed wall

1. Interior view through the panoramic windows
2. Plant containers set in the dining table
3. Custom-made furniture at the public area

1. Entrance
2. Wine tasting bar
3. Host station
4. Main dining area
5. Outdoor smoking terrace
6. Bar
7. Chimney
8. Kitchen

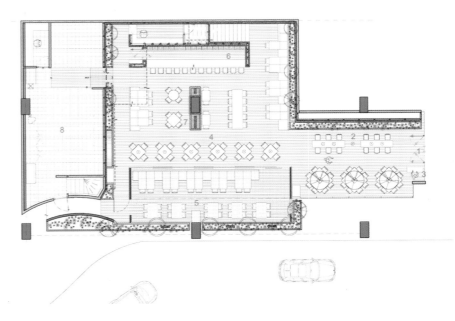

Fuel Station + McDonalds

The vegetation layer, which covers the cantilevered giant canopy of the fuel station adds natural environment and acts as a "ecological shield" for the terrace.

Completion date:
2013
Location:
Batumi, Georgia
Designer:
Khmaladze Architects
Photographer:
Giorgi Khmaladze
Area:
5,000 sqm (Site), 1,200 sqm (Building)

Project Description:

The project is located in one of the newly urbanised parts of the seaside city of Batumi, Georgia. It includes fuels station, McDonald's, recreational spaces and reflective pool.

Given the central location and therefore importance of the site, it was decided to give back as much area as possible for recreation to the city by limiting the footprint of the building and vehicular circulation. This resulted in one volume with all programs compressed within.

Spaces are composed in such way, that two major programs – vehicle services and dining are isolated from one another, both physically and visually so that all operations of fuel station are hidden from the view of the customers of the restaurant.

Because of the predefined, small building footprint, most of the supporting and utility spaces are grouped and located on the ground level to be close to all technical access points.

Public space of the restaurant starts from the lobby and its dedicated entrance on the ground floor. From there, as a way to naturally connect to the upper floor and to offer customers the experience of smooth transition between levels, the floor steps upwards and creates inhabitable decks on intermediate levels to be occupied as dining spaces.

Part of the dining space offers views towards outside water features, while the rest of it seamlessly transitions into open air patio on the upper level. The patio, enclosed from all sides to protect the space from outside noise, provides calm open air seating.

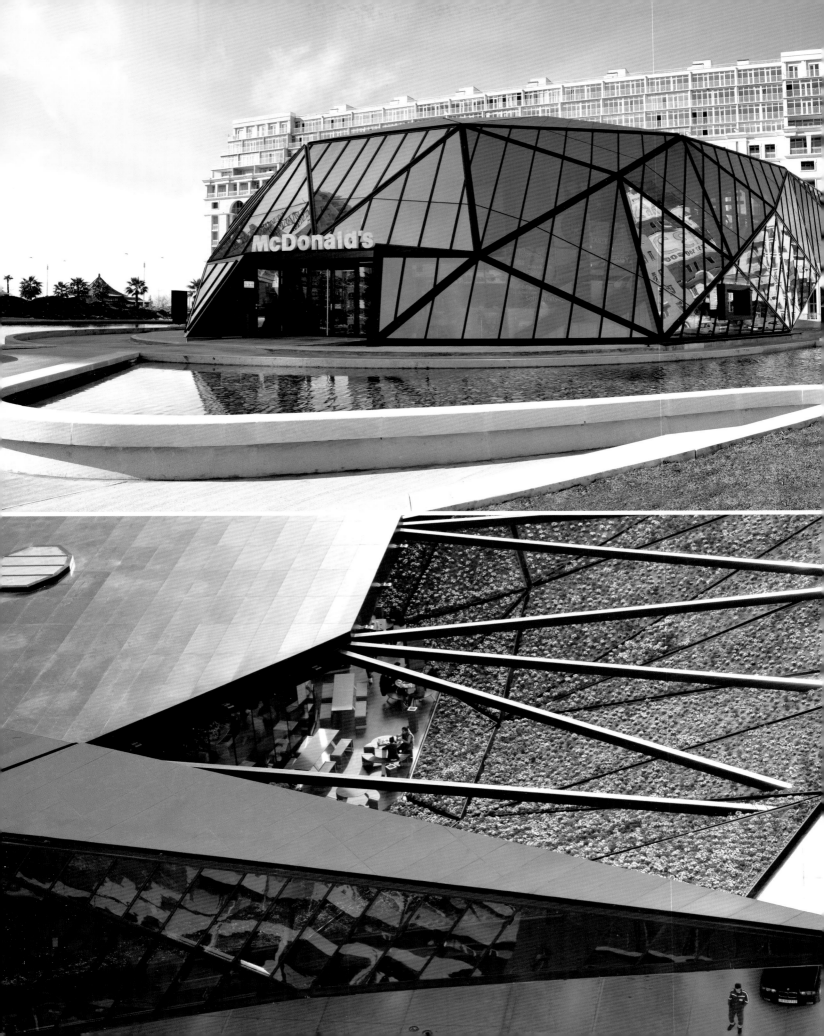

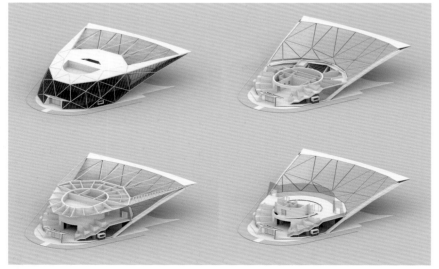

1. The interior plants are divided into geometric patterns, responding to the building exterior

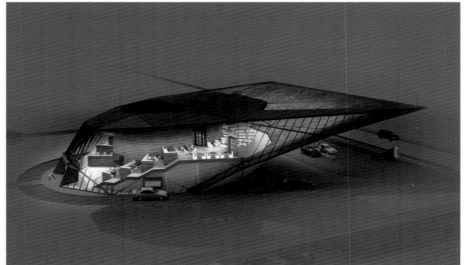

Lizm Hair&Spa

Each private room was subjected to finish with unique features that take advantage of the texture of the material such as old brick and iron plate, vintage flooring, concrete, and Galvalume.

Completion date:
2013
Location:
Shiga, Japan
Designer:
ryo isobe (r.isobe+office for design)
Client:
Hideaki Nakagoshi
Constructor:
Yamashita Engineering
Area:
141 sqm (Floor area)

Project Description:

This is a renovation project of a beauty salon in an old dwelling with shop. The beauty salon is with a cut space of half private room surrounded by waist wall of 1.5m height. And the light of the sun comes through the roof of polycarbonate transparent waiting area.

By making the cut space as a semi-private room, the design significantly reduces the number of seats up to now. The designers were asked to create a space that can provide relaxing space for customers in person. The floor is stacking with the old materials. It also has a transparent roof which will allow more sunlight coming in from the outside.

Private room of the galvanised box jumps out of the existing building. Some private rooms are surrounded by a concrete wall. Some are surrounded by old brick wall. Others are surrounded by black leather iron plate.

Inky shampoo booth is isolated from other areas. Each private room has its own layout and utilises different kinds of materials. By creating the variations of the garden, the design makes a space rich of variation luxuriously.

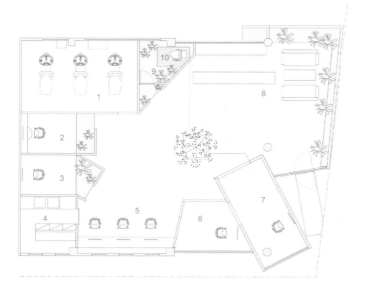

1. Shampoo
2. Cut room 1(VIP)
3. Cut room 2
4. Stock
5. Drink
6. Cut room 3
7. Cut room 4
8. Information
9. Indoor garden
10. WC

1. Information area
2-3. View of the information area from cut room 4
4. Waiting area where the light of the sun coming through the
transparent polycarbonate roof

Meander

The indoor courtyard connecting different areas is the core of design that combines the function of landscaping and ventilation. Thanks to the courtyard, the elderly living in the building have an easy access to nature. They can enjoy the pleasant natural environment indoors, without having to worry about bad weather conditions outdoors. In order to make it resemble real nature maximally, the designers didn't use any pebble or stone to cover the soil in the courtyard. The designers used so less as possible stone to cover the soil in the courtyard.

Completion date:
2006
Location:
Maarheeze, the Netherlands
Designer:
UArchitects (& Aadm)
Photographer:
G. Balvers and J. Sondeyker

Project Description:

At the location of the former shopping centre "de Brink" and where a care home (Marishof) and ten sheltered houses were situated is a new care housing for elder people.

This project exists in four parts.
- 30 houses for seniors (part A) orientated to the square "de Brink" and an extension of the Floralaan divided into 2 to 3 storey.
- 54 residential homes for more elder people (part B) spreading over three storyes situated at the Floralaan and Hagelkruis.
- 30 rooms for elder people who need more treatment and attention (part C) are directed to Hagelkruis and the Lavendelstraat.
- These parts are connected by the "meander" in this order (part D). The meander symbolises the phases of life which the future occupants will follow or experience, seen in time.

The designers have developed a special concrete large brick for this project in the spirit of "Cradle to Cradle", produced not far from the site with low energy cost and can be reused if necessary. The region and the history around Maarheeze (region Eindhoven) are a reason for the use of materials, colours and textures. It is a translation of a historical rural substance into a coded message. This will be visible when intensively studying the building. In small amounts, images of "recognition" come up in the designers' consciousness and because of that, acceptance of relative large extra care housing in a small community is being simplified.

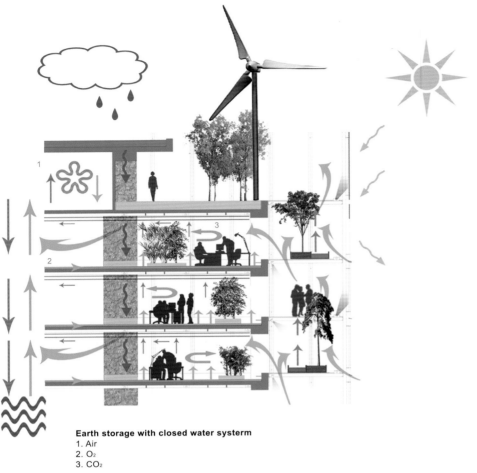

Earth storage with closed water systerm
1. Air
2. O_2
3. CO_2

1. Passage to the first floor
2-3. Indoor garden

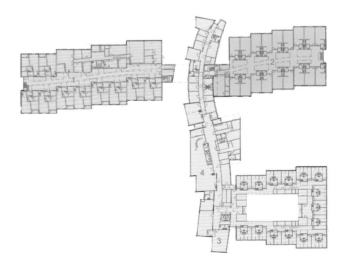

1. 30 houses for seniors
2. 54 residential homes for more elder people
3. 30 rooms for elder people who need more treatment and attention
4. These parts are connected by the "meander" in order

Chapter Six

Interior Landscape Design of Offices

One term called "office landscape" most frequently refers to an interior design concept focused on creating aesthetically pleasing internal office arrangements for corporations. In practice, office landscape involves furniture and desk placement, particularly in open-plan office settings. It often also involves the selection and placement of plants, the creative use of natural light, and the use of artwork to create ambiance. Fig.6.1

Fig.6.1 B+L Pharmaceutical Corporate Office, designed by 137kilo + Beza Projekt. Office furniture with the green wall and trees.

6.1 Office Landscape Increases Work Efficiency

In general, landscaping design can be described as an activity which uses the following elements such as: trees and flowers, as well as, fountains and pools, shrubs and furniture etc. Landscaping is used in both outdoor and indoor spaces. Although, landscaping is different in outdoor and indoor spaces, they are used to create prettier and more pleasant environment/ spaces. If it's hard to work smart in a dumb building, it's also hard to stay healthy in a sick one. Although no one really knows what percentage of health problems are related to building interior quality, there is little doubt that many illnesses, headaches, and eyestrain are directly related to poor lighting, inadequate fresh air, harsh acoustics, and the gloomy surroundings that prevail in many interior spaces. In several studies, when interior landscaping is applied in a building, absence dropped, and sick-leave use was extensively reduced. This suggests that green buildings are not just nicer; they are also healthier as well.

On the other hand, Interiors spaces are the people's daily living-and-working environments. Interior space are designed not only a matter of function, but also of aesthetics and emotional comfort. Therefore, interiors should successfully combine functionality and aesthetically. Landscape is complementary elements of interior volumes. It can be said that, the use of landscape in interior volume helps to create both calm and replenish thus reducing stress.

Pullman, Washington – A study conducted by the College of Agriculture at Washington State University (WSU) shows that live interior plants increase employee productivity and reduce stress.

The study, published in the "Journal of Environmental Horticulture," reports that productivity increased 12 percent when people performed tasks on a computer with plants, compared people who performed the same task in a room without plants.

Productivity was measured by the response time. Professor Virginia Lohr, Ph.D of WSU said, "there was no difference in the number of errors. The big difference was the reaction time, how quickly they pressed the correct key when the plants were present."

"Plants are not just fluff," says Dr. Lohr. "We have felt, and many people who work with plants intuitively believe, that having plants around is vital to our well-being."

Giving office workers some say in the design of their work space gives tremendous benefits in terms of identity realization (see the Prism relationship model, below). Office workers can become "agents of randomness" and gain in other ways as their autonomy is recognised and respected.

Office workers are getting increasingly selective about their work environments and if companies can provide a work space that speaks to issues such as the environment and a humane approach to management, then they stand a good chance of attracting the best employees.

6.2 Having a Garden in the Office

6.2.1 Plant in office
Whilst spacing plants in decorative containers at regular intervals in an office might be considered both practical and stylish, the designer runs the risk of the plants becoming little more respected than the furniture. Conversely, mixtures of plant species, varieties and forms will appear far more natural, as will a variety of foliage styles and colours. Grouping plants together in small clusters and placing them at irregular intervals, instead of regular, grid-like spacing will also look less contrived and more natural.

Recreating the illusion of overlooking a landscape from a position of height can be difficult in an open-plan space, and even harder when dealing with cellular offices or cubicles, but it is not impossible. Depending on the layout of the space concerned, it is possible to create the illusion of overlooking a space by placing tall plants near to the observer and progressively using shorter and shorter plants the further away you get. This makes the actual distance from the observer to the boundary of the space appear further than it really is. The effect can be magnified by bringing the view from beyond the windows into play. Fig.6.2

Fig.6.2 Open architecture and design integrate the work area, lounge area (sofa), dining area and tall trees. The office desks with reserved plant container are space-saving and inject vitality into the space.

Connecting with the outside

First, windows are only there to stop the wind and the rain getting inside, but they often form the boundary of our existence when we are at work – especially if they are furnished with blinds. With a few design tricks, that boundary can be blurred and the outdoors brought in (or the indoors taken out).

Interior landscaping can be designed in a way to draw the eye beyond the window into the outside world. By recruiting a distant focal point - say a tree on the horizon – into the design, the artificial boundary of the window can vanish. In spaces with full-height windows, especially on the ground floor, exterior plants just beyond the window can be used so that the interior and exterior plants become part of the same design, especially if the foliage styles complement each other. Natural spacing of plants either side of the window, perhaps creating a group of plants that ignores the fact of a pane of glass, would be an interesting and effective design. Fig.6.3 and 6.4

Fig.6.3 and 6.4 HDI-Gerling Headquarters, designed by Breimann&Bruun, Hamburg. The heart of the building is the green and airy atrium. The atrium resembles a piazza with reflecting pools which serves all employees and clients alike as a central point of communication.

6.2.2 Space saving plant displays

The benefits of using plants are well known and explained in some depth in this book. But what if you don't have much space to use? Office floor space in some cities is very expensive, so it makes sense to get the most productivity out of it. Where can the plants go?

Small footprints

The latest fashion in plant displays is for tall, narrow containers with shorter plants. Often displayed in pairs, these complement the sleek lines of modern interior furnishings. Typically, these containers have a footprint of less than 30 cm X 30 cm (1 ft X 1 ft), which is similar to that of a waste paper basket. Other examples include narrow troughs with a width of less than 20 cm (8").

The relatively small opening for the plants limits the sizes of plants that can be used. However, displays where the container is taller than the plant still look pleasing. Fig.6.5

Cabinet-top plants

Every office has filing cabinets and cupboards, the tops of which are ideal places for plants. They will help soften the edges of the cabinets and can make the space seem bigger. This is achieved by leading the eye away from the hard top edge of the cabinet and taking it to view the space beyond. In a large office with several ranks of cabinets, the effects can be quite dramatic.

Plant displays for such locations do have their own particular maintenance requirements. Access is not always straightforward and a stepladder may be required. However, irrigation systems built into the plant displays allow watering intervals to be extended to upwards of three weeks.

Cubicle-top plants

Cubicle offices are very common in some parts of the World, especially in North America. Whilst they make efficient use of space and provide a limited amount of privacy for office workers, they can be dull and monotonous. The only view from a cubicle is of the ceiling or through a doorway to anoth-

Fig.6.5 The various plants and containers bring vitality into the office.

er cubicle wall. The spaces between the ranks of cubicles form corridors. These are narrow and do not lend themselves to having floor-standing plant displays, which in any case would not be visible to the vast majority of the occupants of the office space.

The alternative is to use specially made cubicle-top plant containers. A good example is the "Topsiders" range from the USA. These allow plants to be placed on the edges or corners of cubicle walls and provide all cubicle occupants with a plant to call their own. Trailing plants are often used, but there is no reason why a full range of small plants can't be used, including coloured and flowering plants.

As with cabinet-top plants, maintenance of the displays may require the use of a set of steps. However, modern care techniques mean that disruption can be minimised as maintenance intervals can be extended. Fig.6.6 to 6.8

Fig.6.6 Yandex Odessa, Arseniy Borisenko, designed by Peter Zaytsev/za bor architects. The flowerpots are effective in zoning to separate workplaces from corridors, etc. The maritime aesthetics is highlighted by windows, which open a marvelous view to the seaport with its saturate yellow cranes.

Fig.6.7 and 6.8 B+L Pharmaceutical Corporate Office, designed by 137kilo + Beza Projekt.

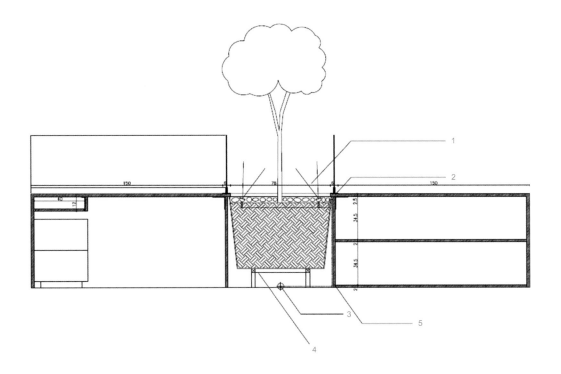

1. Outdoor LED lighting
2. Removable strap C for a possible service of a pot 25 mm x 60 mm
3. Electric/power plug
4. A pot 80cmx80x60
5. Pot's cover 18 mm

Wall-mounted displays

Wall-mounted plant displays are common in corridors and hallways, but also in offices and in places such as restaurants and cafeterias. The most common shape of container is a half-moon and is similar in shape to a lot of uplighters used for illumination. However, more interesting shapes are now available, such as this wall sconce from Australia.

Such plant containers have a limited volume. There is little room for compost and only small plants are appropriate. Another factor to consider is the load bearing capability of the wall. Usually, if the wall is strong enough for a light unit or a picture, then there should not be a problem. However, it is a factor that must always be considered. Fig.6.9 and 6.10

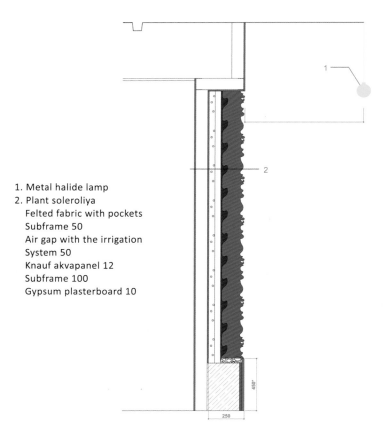

Fig.6.9 Office of Technology company, designed by TSEH Architectural Group.
Ceiling partially remains in its initial pattern – rib panels. From time to time it is broken-up with pipes, wires and other communications. And finally the ceiling transforms into the wooden waves and continues as bionic bench, which floats under the floor and appears a center of guest area. This area could be used as cinema hall, training room and master classes platform. Involvement and cross spreading are the main features of the project.
Main expression of "New life" became green which appears on different surfaces and in various interpretations everywhere. These are vertical green columns near reception desk, green cube right in the middle of the office floor, green wall-fence by entrance, shrubs spring through the metal terrace, green hills with trees growing through the concrete floor surface and green glades on the roof.

Fig. 6.10 Details of the green wall.

1. Metal halide lamp
2. Plant soleroliya
   Felted fabric with pockets
   Subframe 50
   Air gap with the irrigation
   System 50
   Knauf akvapanel 12
   Subframe 100
   Gypsum plasterboard 10

Desktop displays

Desktops are often the only personal space office workers can claim and customise to their own preferences. Many people bring in their own "pet plants" but there is no reason why professionally installed and maintained displays can't be accommodated. There is now a wide range of good quality plants and containers that are ideal for desktops that will complement corporate colour schemes and design styles as well as providing a benefit to the staff in the building. Fig.6.11

By the way, there is some evidence that office staff will take greater pride in their workspace if they are given a greater say in the choice of furnishings, fittings and decoration (including plants).

Fig.6.11 Residential Center Cugat Natura, designed by JFARQUITECTES, 2012.

Plant screens and room dividers

The space in open plan offices is frequently divided by screens, either to provide a limited amount of privacy or to segregate different functions within the space. These screens are often ugly and can be expensive. Some screens are available that incorporate plants into their design. Fig.6.12 to 6.16

Fig.6.12 Barra & Barra Office, designed by Damilanostudio Architects. The plants serve as the divider of two office areas, which shifts people's eyesight from walls to the pleasant greenery.

Fig.5.13 The "Google Office" ™ – a living plant screen designed by Futurespace. The plant screen formed by pots and frames not only provides better privacy for the Google Australian office environment, but blocks the noise interruption from other areas of the building.

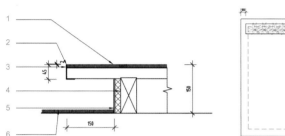

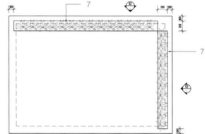

1. Floor finish to platform as specified
2. Top angle to be 2mm below carpet pile
3. Flat aluminum angle with countersunk flat head screw fixings to platform edge spaced evenly along edges of platform @ centres to suit. Bronze
anodized fixing and angle to match partition framing
4. 110×50mm timber stud base support spaced every 450mm CNTRS
5. Bronze anodized skirting to match partition skirtings
6. Timber/carpet flooring as specified
7. Plant wall

Fig.6.14 to 6.16 Section Details

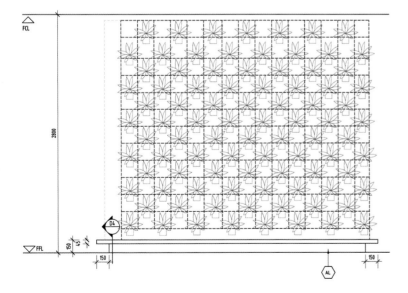

Views into atriums

If there really is no room for plants in the office, then try to ensure that everyone has a view of some greenery. Atriums are often overlooked by offices and these spaces are ideal for plant displays.

Barra&Barra Office

The choice of materials, chrome and transparent walls widens her eyes to the concept of office as a space is transformed resulting in a closed space where the gaze is lost over the walls to the green lawns.

Completion date:
2012
Location:
Centallo, Italy
Designer:
Damilanostudio Architects
Photographer:
Andrea Martiradonna
Area:
490 sqm

Project Description:

The "Barra Barra Office" was born as an expression of the spirit of the company at your side that cares about the eco-energy saving and new philosophy and technologies in construction and business management.

The result is a space, which despite being in an industrial building, related to nature. A young and dynamic environment characterised by vegetation that grows in beds raised so as to give the feeling of find immersed. In this place of the green jersey are executive offices, sales offices, technical offices, relaxation areas and an exhibition hall.

The energy optimisation is ensured by an advanced home automation system with systems interfaced to the web server allowing full remote management of systems through tablets and smartphones.

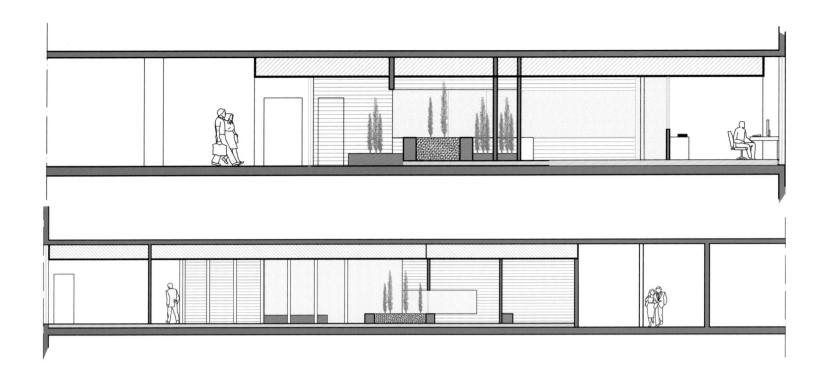

1. Plants are arranged between the sales and administrative offices
2. The large windows provide better view of the garden from the offices
3. The green reception desk echoes with the plants

TECHNICAL AREA

1. Warehouse
2. Technical room
3. Exhibition
4. Meeting room
5. Sell
6. Laundry
7. Cafeteria
8. Printers
9. Waiting
10. Reception
11. Technical area
12. Buying
13. Administration
14. Marketing
15. Indoor garden

1. Planting bed in the office
2-3. Creating a microclimate in the office
4-5. Tidy and elegant interior design

Office Greenhouse

In cabinets – walls which are with windows on open-space room, Timorous Beasties wallpaper London Toile is used, which are common to green concept and in which are portrayed witty scenes from London.

Completion date:
2012
Location:
Riga, The Republic of Latvia
Design:
OPEN Architecture and Design
Photographer:
Maris Lagzdins
Area:
170 sqm

Project Description:

The keyword of design for office Greenhouse is greenery – principal wish of client was plenty of herbage. The specifics of work in this office gave a possibility to make open-space office, planning special cabinets only for few groups of employees. In open-space area we designed multifunctional piece of furniture in which is integrated working places, rest area (sofa), dining zone and big sized trees. Kitchen is made of 6mm thin metal sheet, integrating metal sink and pull-out rubbish bin. The rest of kitchen wall is greened by flowerpots which are put on warehouse wall-shelves, straightened on rails. Wall construction is left visible from side of open-space room, using plasterboard plates only from cabinet side, so form open-space we can see construction profiles. Walls are painted white and in some planes the brick is left in its natural look.

1-3. Details of the plants
4. View of the office area
5. Simple design of the interior landscape

1. Office
2. Chillout
3. Cabinet
4. Cabinet
5. Cabinet
6. Kitchen

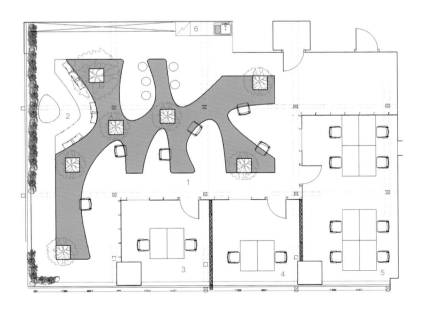

207

NBG i-bank Store

As these projects show, even the most densely populated urban centers can be turned into green oases by using the right solutions and materials.

Completion date:
2011
Location:
Athens, Greece
Designer:
Vitaverde
Photographer:
Vitaverde
Area:
25 sqm

Project Description:

The First Vertical Gardens in Greece

The first vertical gardens built in Thessaloniki and Athens, Greece are located at the I-Bank stores of the National Bank of Greece. It was Vitaverde that created the first vertical gardens in a very interesting and challenging project, which has been realised in a new environment and philosophy developed by the NBG. This electronic banking facility offers self-service e-banking as well as space for relaxation and entertainment, and the vertical gardens perfectly fit the modern architectural design and the high-tech surroundings.

The plants in the living wall purify the interior air, minimise stress, and increase productivity of the employees. Clients enjoy relaxing while having a break in the coffee corner where the garden is situated, and the overall aesthetics of the space has been improved in a unique way.

Presenting the possibilities of creating more innovative solutions, the gardens bring their healthy contribution to the environment and they are also a reason to believe that vision can be turned into reality. With a design of organic forms and a visual combination of textures and colours, the gardens fit gently in the general feel of the I-Bank stores.

These projects were the start of many similar projects where working environments are being decorated with innovative green solutions, leading to a greener urban environment for the citizens of Greek cities.

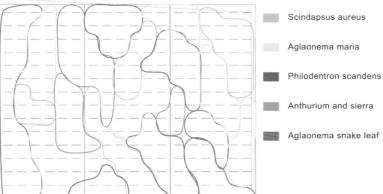

Scindapsus aureus

Aglaonema maria

Philodentron scandens

Anthurium and sierra

Aglaonema snake leaf

1. Virtual and real greenery
2. Extraordinary space for self-service banking
3. Plants increase motivation and positive energy
4. Green light at the end of the tunnel
5. Relaxing area and living wall

1. Nephrolepis exaltata Boston
(Boston fern)
2. Pellea rotundifolia
3. Spathiphyllum
4. Chlorophytum ocean
5. Maranta leaconeura
6. Aglaonema maria
7. Fittonia green
8. Philodendrom imperial green
9. Chamaedorea elegans
10. Calathea rubibarba
11. Ficus repens
12. Fittonia red

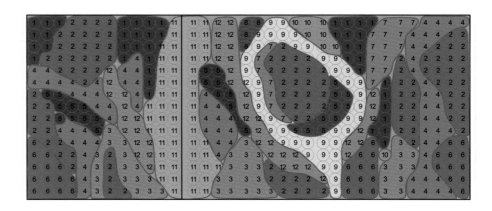

Madrid Idom Office

An atmosphere closer to that of a household which would do away with the axioms of the traditional office building. A space free from false ceilings and floors and with wood carpentry, cloth ducts, bare masonry walls, slow propulsion of air at room temperature and operational windows…in a nut shell: the non – office.

Completion date:
2010
Location:
Madrid, Spain
Designer:
ACXT
Architects:
Jorge Martínez Bermejo,
Jesús María Susperregui
Photographer:
Fernando Guerra
Area:
15,300 sqm

Project Description:

BUILDING THE NON – OFFICE
The HVAC based on radiant systems (TABS), uses the high thermal inertia of the structure and its post-tensioned concrete floor slabs. An air propulsion system is conceived exclusively for slow air renovation through cloth ducts, which can be cleaned and which avoids noise pollution.

The great structural spans allow for a smooth and flexible flow area. Sun protection faces towards the south, and is toned down light from the north. The perception of a continuous space runs both horizontally and vertically to form a setting that includes fragments of nature, hanging gardens and green walls. A correct strategy for reusing water makes the most of it for visual and acoustic pleasure.

AIR RENOVATION
Air is renewed in a much calmer way, since temperature is no longer an issue, by means of a shifting textile ducts system. It is a technology that has its origin in the food industry due to its high hygienic and sanitary levels, never before having been applied to an office building project in Spain.

NATURAL VENTILATION
The use of a natural ventilation system, without any mechanical aid, has been researched. To that purpose, vertical communication atriums have been planned, working as great HVAC return air collectors, dispensing with conventional return ducts.

The envelope of the building incorporates a

series of design elements aimed toward the minimization of the energy demand: high thermal insulation, high quality glass, exceptional solar protection and double vegetable skin both in the façade and the cover, among others.

VEGETABLE COVER
It diminishes the solar charge received by the building, thus regulating the temperature of the surface exposed to the sun. It retains water and reduced the "heat island" effect.

South and west façades is protected against solar radiation by means of a steel structure that supports a vegetable cover. In summer, the leaves prevent direct radiation from going through, and in winter the lack of leaves allows for a better lighting in the interior.

COVER
The water is collected in the building cover, channeled toward the gutter in the South facade and lead toward the patios.

SOUTH FAÇADE
The water collected is channeled between the metallic skin and the glass, thus being used once the cycle for the vegetable irrigation has been completed.

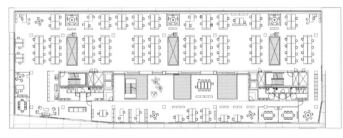

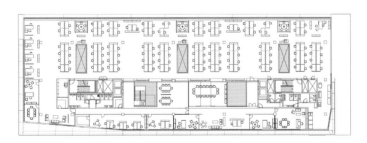

1. The tree in Lobby
2. Details of the garden

PLENUM

In the ground floor, a false bottom allows for the housing of a water storage system made of several water layers and interconnected wells.

WATER COLLECTION AND REDISTRIBUTION

Due to the semiarid climate of Madrid (only 436mm of precipitation per year), the optimum usage of the available water is crucial to attain the highest energetic and environmental goals.

The water accumulated in the water reserves located under the ground floor generates around itself a space of vegetation which contributes to the temperature regulation of exterior zones during the summer. 100% of the water accumulated is treated and reused both for the irrigation system and for the use and treatment of sanitary waters. It is also used in the structure's cooling system by evaporation.

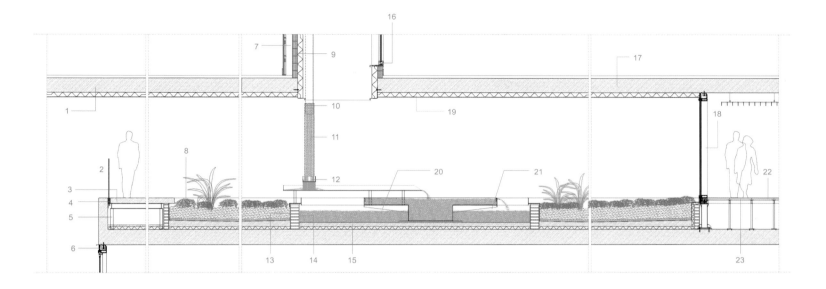

1. Acrylic mortar THK=6mm
   Expanded polystyrene insulation THK=12cm
   Post tensioned concrete slab
2. 10+10 mm laminated glass handrail
3. Concrete composite slab, polished finish, THK = 15cm.
4. Galvanised steel handrail fixing piece
5. Reinforced concrete wall from phenolic formwork panels,
   THK = 25cm
   Galvanized steel substructure Mortar compression layer,
   Min THK = 5cm
   Extruded polystyrene insulation
   THK=8cm
   Post tensioned concrete slab
6. Anodised aluminium curtain wall
   Raisable sliding door
   High performance glass: 8/16/5+5 low emissivity coating
   and 90% argon filled
7. Double 15mm plasterboard inner cladding.
   Galvanized steel profiles.
   46 mm studs every 60cm
8. Polyurethane sheet ,waterproofing, THK=2mm
   Topsoil Geotextile fabric Expanded clay aggregate
   Slopingmortar bed
9. Honeycomb clay block
   THK = 19cm Expanded polystyrene insulation
   THK=12cm Acrylic mortar
   THK=6mm
10. Drainpipe
    Stainless steel lower finishing profile.
    THK= 4mm
11. Methacrylate cylindrical tube
12. Stainless steel PFC (C-profile with a lid)
    Stainless steel PFC (parallel flange channel)
    Rain-water collecting gutter. 3mm stainless steel
13. 1 brick-thick cored brick masonry wall, screeded and with formwork
    Polyurethane sheet waterproofing, THK=2mm
14. Post tensioned concrete slab, THK=42cm
15. Extruded polystyrene insulation, THK=8cm
    Sloping mortar bed

16. Solid syroco woodwork.
    Lacquered MDF skirting board.
    Steel counterframe #40.40.3
    Honerycomb clay block, THK = 19cm
    Post tensioned concrete slab, THK=40cm
17. Flooring made up by 8 cm semi-dry mortar screed
    and a 5 mm
    polyurethane multi-layer paving with a glazed finish.
    Post tensioned concrete slab, THK=40cm
    Expanded polystyrene insulation, THK=12cm
    Acrylic mortar, THK=6mm
18. Anodized aluminium curtain wall
    High performance glass:
    8/16/5+5 low emissivity coating and 90% argon
    filled.
    Bamboo timber lattice. 100x10 cm slats every 15cm
19. Expanded polystyrene insulation, THK=12cm
    Acrylic mortar, THK=6mm
20. Upper basin of rain-water pond. 8 mm stainless
    steel sheet
    5 mm stainless steel gusset plates
21. Basin 5 mm stainless steel sheet
    Base 8 mm stainless steel sheet
    Main body 5 mm stainless steel sheet
    Side edge 8 mm stainless steel sheet
    Pond edge 6 mm stainless steel sheet
22. Short wool fitted carpet
    Raised flooring panel: galvanized steel encapsulated
    chipboard,
    THK = 4cm
23. Raised flooring substructure
     Galvanized steel profiles

1. Water garden

TBWA / Hakuhodo

Because of a lack of natural light, KDa paid special attention to lighting, cunningly re-cladding the beams with integrated lighting and air-conditioning. Their care has borne fruit – the plants in the office are growing rapidly!

Completion date:
2008
Location:
Tokyo, Japan
Designer:
Klein Dytham architecture
Photographer:
Kozo Takayama
Area:
4,215sqm

Project Description:

This project is the Tokyo HQ of a joint venture between TBWA, an innovative global advertising agency, and Hakuhodo, one of Japan's largest ad firms, and was built in a disused bowling alley that KDa discovered in a multistorey amusement complex. KDa conceived of the office interior as a park and filled it with plants, boardwalks, and green shagpile carpet. Scattered across this landscape is a miniature village. These shelters serve as meeting rooms, project rooms, and director's offices, and some have been fitted with ladders that allow staff to climb onto their roofs to find a relaxed spot for meetings or a break. The bowling alley's column-free space allowed the office to be laid out freely, but the building's bowling lane DNA showed through in the down-stand beams on the ceiling,

so this dynamic was incorporated to give a subtle order to the layout of the office landscape.

When the existing ceiling was removed the bowling alley became a double-height space, and the 2m-deep down-stand beams that span the full width of the floor were revealed. As a column-free space, the bowling alley allowed complete freedom in laying out the office – anything was possible! The powerful rhythm of the beams suggested arranging the desks and circulation zones in a pattern that re-established the original dynamic of the bowling lanes. The wide-open space, however, inspired KDa to imagine the office as a park, so they filled it with fun "landscape" elements. The park combines both real and

Section

1. The narrow alley connects the offices in a clever way
2. A boardwalk runs through the centre of the office, with plants grown by the glass door

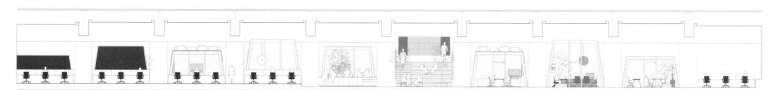

Section

Plan of the office

1:300

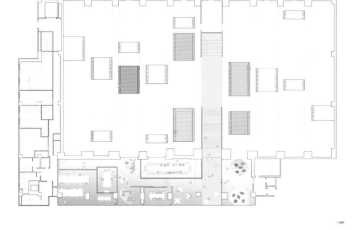

1:300

fake greenery – living plants and green shag-pile carpet. A boardwalk runs through the centre of the office, and a series of "pocket parks" have been arranged beside the windows.

Scattered across the floor are a series of shelters that serve as meeting rooms, project rooms, and director's offices. The shelters have been decorated with a pattern whose meaning is deliberately ambiguous – it suggests both the icing on a cake and the snow on Mt. Fuji, and was chosen to inject another element of fun and light-hearted charm into the space. Some of the shelters have been fitted with ladders, allowing the staff to climb onto their roofs to find a relaxed spot for meetings, brainstorming, a break, or a picnic – from these rooftops, staff have a view over the whole office! The shelters subtly divide the space occupied by the office's 340 staff into intimate neighborhoods connected by narrow lanes. The result is that the space doesn't feel like a corporate office, but like a little village in its own landscape.

With the project's super-deep plan, KDa paid special attention to building services, carrying out a number of technical studies.

Chapter Seven

Landscape Design of Living Environment

7.1 Landscape Design of Living Environment

Homes somewhat short of perfection – window views may be bleak or uninspiring; kitchens and bathroom, for all their functionalism, may seem cold or antiseptic. Even the most elegantly appointed living rooms may lack vitality and visual warmth. However, add a lush window, a pot rack dripping in herbs and saucepans, or a jungle of decorative foliage and an ornamental specimen tree – in short, an indoor garden – and the impact is immediate and dramatic. A stark interior can become a verdant landscape, warmed by tropical greenery, alive with design possibilities limited only by the imagination and dedication of the indoor gardener or professional interior landscape designer.

A well-planned interior landscape can reflect personality and create just the right mood, whether you want to dazzle or soothe, astonish or delight. There's a world of difference between buying a few plants from the grocery store to place randomly here or there and planning an indoor garden meant to complement, enhance or modify existing interior design. A successful indoor garden combines the principles of interior decorating with sound horticultural practices. It's possible to create growing, ever-changing landscape in every house.

Foliage plants offer a fantastic opportunity – they can dramatically change the appearance of a ho-hum room into one filled with life and appear. Imaginatively used, plants not only create a stunning display, but they can also provide a simple and economical way to solve interior decorating problems. The varied foliage of house plants adds pattern and color, modified straight lines and softens harsh areas. Of course we use plants for their beauty, but there are numerous other uses for foliage plants in an indoor environment.

Use of houseplants:
• correct architectural problems
• separate a large room into different living areas
• shorten the apparent length of a long, narrow room
• fill awkard corner by softening sharp edges
• create an effect of drama

- provide an unusual focal point
- provide more oxygen for cleaner air
- bring nature indoors

Colour, size, lighting requirements and temperature will all be considered. If Indoor gardening can be taken up on a more grand scale by including a special room or greenhouse in the building plans or using an existing room with lots of good light. On a smaller scale, many can garden indoors on a kitchen windowsill, a steamy bathroom or any other well-lighted room. Plus, if there is a spot where plants will help to solve a problem, "grow lights" can be installed.

7.2 Plan, Scale and Placement

When planning the location of an indoor landscape, look at the various areas available. The indoor landscape, like an outdoor landscape, should allow space for plantings, ornamentation and sculptural features. Unlike outdoor areas that require changing shapes, you need to utilise available spaces like corners, nooks and passageways. Look at the traffic patterns of inhabitants to locate an appropriate space for the indoor landscape. Consider the size and weight of the landscape, and be sure adequate support is available. Plan the design so all areas are easily accessible for maintenance. Fig.7.1 and 7.2

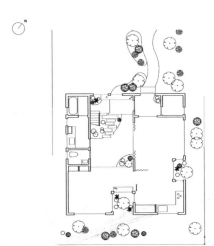

Fig.7.1 and 7.2 Kofunaki House, designed by ALTS DESIGN OFFICE. The interior adopts an open-style layout, promoting indoor garden of small trees and shrubs at of all available areas including stairs, corners and entrances. Gravel is used at the top of the compost, matched with wood panels.

Scale is all-important in indoor landscape design: a towering Ficus bejamina (weeping fig) would dwarf a small den; likewise, a solitary fern would be lost in a spacious living room. The experts suggest using single specimen plants to make a statement – they are usually larger, more stable species, with a lot of drama. One exception is hanging plants – from a design perspective, two smaller hanging plants, grouped together, with varying height, offer more impact than a larger hanging plant hanging alone.

Creative placement of plants in your home can transform nondescript alcoves and niches, halls and stairways, and visually brighten "dead" areas such as fireplaces in summertime. Even an empty wall becomes a design asset when used in indoor garden planning.

As a design element, foliage plants can soften the look of a room and help disguise architectural defects; a specimen tree or plant grouping could visually separate an open-plan living and dining area, for instance, or a high-beam ceiling could be "lowered" with hanging plants. On the other hand, improperly placed plants will accentuate trouble spots. Fig.7.3

Fig.7.3 GARDEN PATIO, designed by Jeroen Schipper Architecten. The kitchen, dining area, lounge area, collection room, office area and swimming pool are connected by the indoor garden, softening the linear layout.

Windows, of course, are a natural site for plants. Use plants here to create a break from indoors to outdoors, or use a tiered foliage grouping to make undesirable window views recede. Try to link interior to exterior by matching indoor plants with those grown directly outside your window. Give bay windows or glass walls the treatment they deserve, installing plants of important size, grouped with an eye for overall effect. Resist the urge to clutter such valuable sun-lit space with a myriad of tiny-potted specimens.

7.3 Inner Courtyard

A courtyard inside of the house is a quite unusual thing but it's a perfect solution to create a private relaxing area. It gives you the feel of the outdoors but nobody could see you there. A courtyard is a small, secluded indoor area accessed via the home. The design of an interior courtyard garden takes advantage of the enclosure to exhibit vertical plantings, group together large, potted plants and include sculptural elements for visual interest.

It isn't necessary to give up a precious room in the house, consider converting a connecting area of the house into a natural haven, such as a hallway or reception area; a little oasis like these provides a beautiful divide between living spaces, and promotes a sense of peace. Fig.8.4 and 8.5

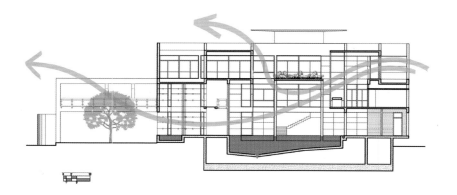

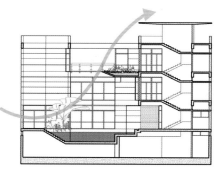

Fig 7.4 and 7.5 S.A Residence, designed by SHATOTTO architecture for green living. The site is surrounded by multi-storeyed buildings as on-lookers. An introverted design strategy was hence adopted, placing a water-court as a swimming pond in the middle of the house to ensure privacy. The south and south east have been designed to bring in cool breeze during the hot, humid summers and the warmth of the sun during the winters. The central water court acts as a natural exhaust system, allowing hot air to escape and making the middle court a cool sanctuary.

Garden Patio

The main volume is moved to the back of the site, its closed parts being as close to the neighbours as possible. As a result, the house enjoys a lot of free space to admire its own garden that flows down to the green mass of the park, creating a single green space.

Completion date:
2007
Location:
Kharkov, Ukraine
Designer:
Oleg Drozdov, Aleksandr Strulev
Landscape designer:
Jeroen Schipper Architecten
Photographer:
Andrey Avdeenko
Area:
513 sqm

Project Description:

The plot is situated on an active slope, on the border between private residential development and botanical garden. The layout strategy proposes maximum contact with the park by exploiting the view from all internal spaces. It was essential to highlight the active terrain by means of landscape elements and volumes.

The composition consists of two cubes – the manor and the garage unit with guestrooms on top – which are threaded on the line of a glazed passage. The garden and the internal spaces enjoy utmost protection from the outer environment.

The life of the house is influenced by as many as four gardens.

First is the city botanical garden. The manor enjoys a wonderful view of its green groves lying below.

Besides, the house has its own sloping garden. Four elegant rectangular terraces highlight the difference between the levels, presenting a peculiar contrast with the natural landscape. Different orientation of terraces creates a dynamic connection between the house and its surrounding. The terraces grow wider as they descend the hill creating more usable space. On the whole, the site has a more open nature in comparison with the green mass lying below.

Terraces make a characteristic feature of the house. The main volume is surrounded by two

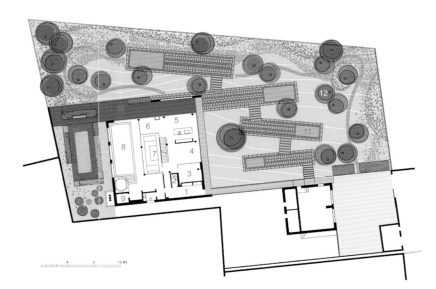

1. Blooming plants are kept at the plant containers in the rectangular terrace
2. View of the indoor garden from the first floor
3. The square atrium is surrounded by glass walls
4. The atrium next to the stairs

rows of wooden terraces. The one which overlooks the botanical garden is shielded by a plane with a window. On a hot summer day it makes a comfortable place for having meals on the open air.

The third garden is a real secret garden – a cozy nook, shrouded in mystery and romance. One can get into this chamber garden only via the terrace formed by the difference in layers.

The fourth garden is a green heart of the house. The patio garden is situated in the very core of the multifunctional living space, which represents an ideal square. Around the winter garden there is a sequence of zones, each having its own function: kitchen, dining room, lounge, collection of traditional Russian samovars, office and swimming pool. The members of the family can be in different zones but at the same time stay in one single common space. Visual connections between all internal spaces intersect the layer of the winter garden with tropical plants. The winter garden also plays a major role in the gallery of the first floor where the bedrooms are situated.

1. Hall
2. Bathroom
3. Study
4. Living room
5. Kitchen
6. Dining room
7. Winter garden
8. Swimming pool
9. Sauna
10. Terrace
11. Bedroom
12. Wardrobe

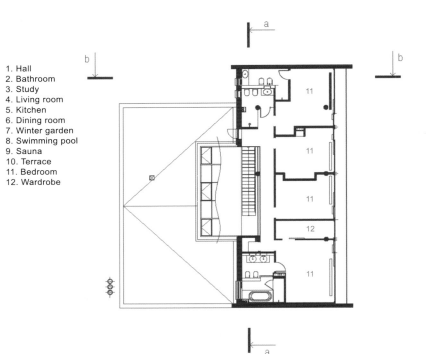

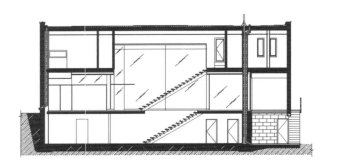

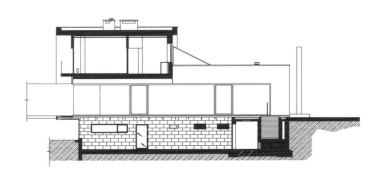

1. View of the indoor garden, which sits at the heart of the building, can be enjoyed from all angles
2. The selected large plants help create a refreshing interior

S.A Residence

It is the inter-relationship between form and void which is at the heart of Lalon's philosophy, the underlying inspiration for this building. The open quad at the centre depicts Nothingness.

Completion date:
2011
Location:
Dhaka, Bangladesh
Design firm:
SHATOTTO architecture for green living
Photographer:
Daniele Domenicali
Area:
1,920 sqm

Project Description:

Water, channelises its expansive existence subtly inside the weave of life, mingling toil and poetry into the land of Bangladesh.

During Monsoon the 52 rivers that carry water across Bangladesh inundate two-thirds of the land. The water recedes, leaving behind fertile alluvial soil, transforming the landscape into large patches of paddy fields. Lalon, the 18th-century mystic minstrel of this land said, "If one thing is not there inside the body then it is not outside the body either."

The human form has two parts — body, being the shell and thoughts as the soul. Shell and Soul are interdependent, yet independent; belonging to each other while belonging to themselves. Architecture is similar, with the building envelope as the shell and nature as the soul.

The building envelope of this three-storey residence is a pure square, constructed of a single material, cast-concrete. Considering the socio-economic conditions of Dhaka, architectural vocabulary is kept simple, with traditional spaces like the courtyard, pond, ghat (steps to water) and ample green to merge together urban and rural typologies in this urban context.

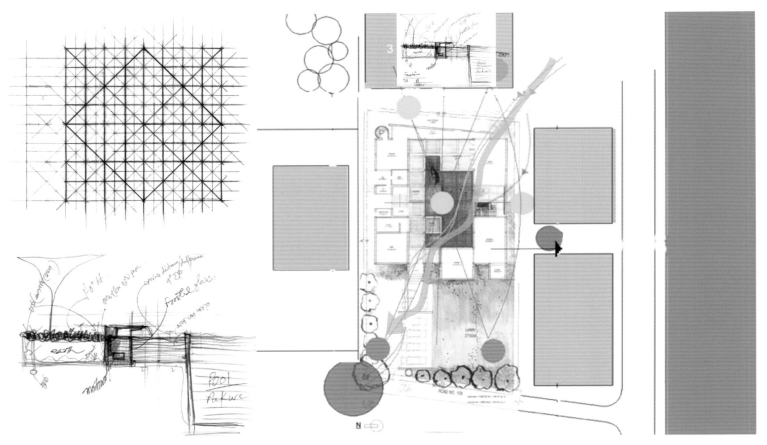

Conceptual sketches site plan

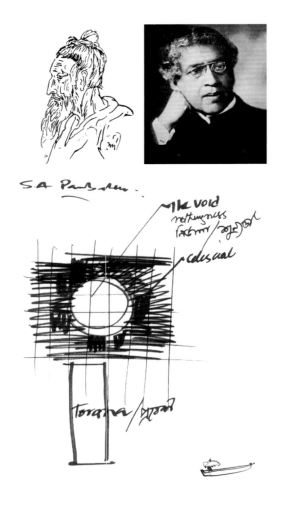

The site is surrounded by multi-storeyed buildings as on-lookers. An introverted design strategy was hence adopted, placing a water-court as a swimming pond in the middle of the house to ensure privacy.

The south and southeast have been designed to bring in cool breeze during the hot, humid summers and the warmth of the sun during the winters. The central water court acts as a natural exhaust system, allowing hot air to escape and making the middle court a cool sanctuary.

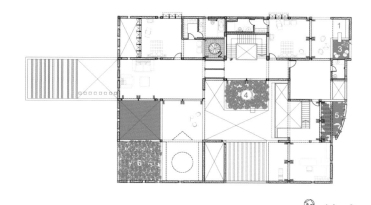

Second Floor Plan
1. Terrace
2. Rocks/gravels
3. Garden
4. Crop field
5. Bamboo bush
6. Jungle

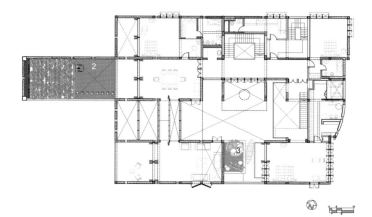

First Floor Plan
1. Jungle
2. Reflection pool
3. Forest below

1. Concrete, structural clarity and aesthetic simplicity
2. Shell and nature
3. Conversations with green

Ground Floor Plan
1. Garden
2. Wooden bridge
3. Swimming pond
4. Lawn
5. Jungle

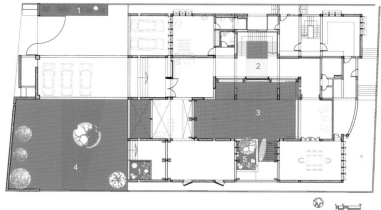

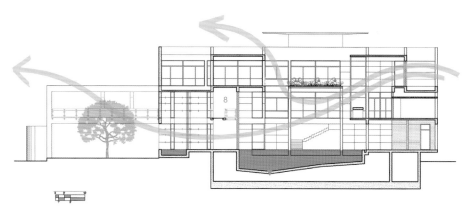

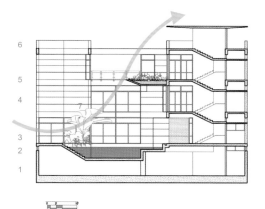

1. Basement
2. Road level
3. Ground floor
4. 1st floor
5. 2nd floor
6. 3rd floor
7. Hijal tree/ barringtonia acutangula
8. Glass bridge

1. Water courtyard of the house, also a swimming pond
2. View of the water courtyard from the interior

3x9 House

Thus, 3x9 House can be said that nature is skilfully to any corners of the house by creating "connecting space" which bridges and adjusts the different domains and places, from outside to the ground floor and the first floor.

Completion date:
2012
Location:
Hochiminh city, Vietnam
Designer:
a21studio
Photographer:
Hiroyuki Oki
Area:
27 sqm

Project Description:

Even in Hochiminh, a chaotic and highly density city, a 3 m wide and 9 m deep plot in a narrow street is still considered as a thorny problem for renovating an old house to a more comfortable and functional space. The house is designed for a middle age woman and her friend, who are inspired by music and beauty of nature.

The modesty and cleanliness are the first impressions of the house look. Horizontal louvers embellished with some flowers give distinction but not strange to its exterior in compare with neighbours.

The ground floor seems to be larger and tidier because of the combination of living room, dinner, and kitchen without any partitions to define the spaces. The familiar materials such as bricks and steels are used flexibly to add raw feeling to these man-made spaces. Moreover, nature is delivered into the house by the introduction of a tree right at the entrance. This tree, as a living body, not only softens rough sides of the design but also connect the ground space to the upper space.

The first floor with the same language is the space where bedroom and toilet are located, emphasize the rich of daylight due to its openness to the sky. The connection between bedroom and toilet is collection of sparse wooden pieces, which cause flows of light, wind, rain and even human intentions among the house. This is also the place where the tree meets its need for sunlight.

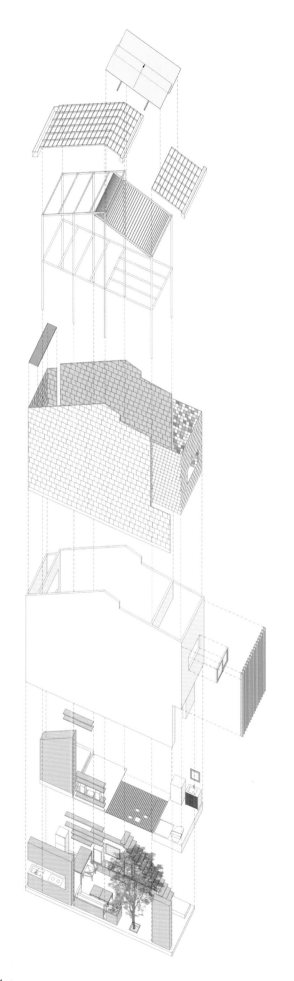

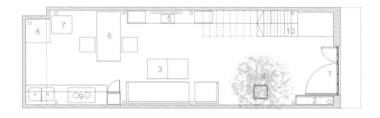

1. Main entrance
2. Shoes self
3. Living room
4. The averrhoa carambola
5. Music player
6. Dining table
7. Refrigerator
8. Cleaning floor
9. Kitchen
10. Wooden stair
11. Wooden floor

12. Bed
13. Bookshelf
14. Wardrobe
15. Steel frame void
16. Lounge chair
17. Bath tub
18. Washing machine
19. Basin
20. Toilet
21. Exterior louvers

1. View of building from the street

2. Details of the façade

3. Open design of the living and dining area

4. Wall below the stairs serves as the TV backdrop

Windmills of Your Mind

All roads and driveways are in hand dressed cobblestones, wood and glass pergolas serve as the covers over the car porticos and landscaping itself is used as a material – in the form of vertical creeper panels and grass covered structures.

Completion date:
under construction
Location:
Bangalore, India
Designer:
Shibanee & Kamal Architects
Photographer:
Shibanee & Kamal Architects
Area:
1,625 sqm

Project Description:

In the city of Bangalore, large housing projects are a fairly new concept. Most of the citizens still prefer an individual residence on a private plot of land. The challenge for the designers therefore, was to design a housing project in which the units did not feel like flats – as they are popularly called – but like intimate homes – with the warmth of a garden, personalised spaces and an overall scale that would not be intimidating.

The 24 acre property for this project is situated on the edge of a small lake in the heart of India's Silicon Valley – Bangalore, and is designed mainly with the well-travelled "Global Indian" professional in mind. The programme for the development of 1.75 million sft includes seven 19 storey towers comprising 152 simplex units of 2500 sft each, 160 duplex units of 5924 sft & 20 triplex units of 7648 sft,

and a cluster of 73 earth sheltered villas, with a central community space which has large green areas interspersed with a dense cluster of trees.

The Villas
The 73 earth covered villas have been designed to create an intimate scale, with the idea that the streetscape should not be dominated with the monotony of built volumes sticking out on both sides of the street. Therefore, with the help of the existing contours of the land, and by creating split levels inside the villas, taking part of the structure half a floor lower than the road, and keeping the front portion of the home designed at a single level – the designers have been able to ensure that, for a person walking or driving down the street, all the homes appear as single storey homes despite the fact that they are actually

all two-storeyed. The low car portico (only around 8' from the cobbled driveway) and the gently curved landscaped roofs further help achieve the intimate scale. Each villa also has a vegetable garden on the roof of the living room.

The floor plan of each individual home is L-shaped and the L is placed along one edge of the plot – thus ensuring a large green space inside the L and also ensuring that every room has a view of the garden. This also eliminates small passages between homes. With four units mirrored and placed back-to-back, the total number of visible structures reduces to one quarter – so, though there are 67 villas, there are only 17 visible structures thereby removing the clutter. This also creates a central space between 4 villas where only tall plants have been used for separation – no walls.

The Duplex apartments

Challenging the perception that apartments can't really get you the same feel as an individual home, these units are designed with large gardens (70' x 14'), a water body and wood deck within each unit. Every living space including the kitchen, is adjacent to the garden, separated only by large glass paneled sliding doors, always providing the feeling of being close to nature – even on higher floors. The gardens are complete with sprinklers and a drip irrigation system and with plants as tall as 16 feet. Upstairs, the family space opens out onto a glass deck that allows light to pass through to the wood deck below it. With double height spaces, a large library, an aquarium between the kids' bathroom and bedroom, large wood deck and tall bamboos in the garden, most visitors to the prototype of this unit are unable to believe that this could be on the 17th floor.

The long water body, running along the entire length of the apartment, acts like a safety feature – preventing young ones from getting too close to the balcony edge. The large overhangs created by the garden slabs shade the glazing from direct sun – keeping the interiors cool.

The apartment blocks have been placed next to each other in a straight line, thereby avoiding views from one apartment into another and also providing maximum number of units a view of the lake and the green roofs of the villas – which are a treat to look at – adding to the scenic views towards the lake. This way the apartments are also far enough from the villas so as not to be intrusive. The rooftops of the seven towers have been connected by a skywalk above the 19th floor and designed to be completely landscaped with dwarf trees and cobbled streets. Vibrant with plants and city views, the skywalk is ideal for morning or evening walks or for jogging. The edges have been designed with railings that slope outward – preventing kids from climbing onto them and also providing privacy to the triplex units below.

Natural materials have been used throughout the project to create intimacy with nature. All external walls are built in high quality exposed terracotta bricks sourced from the neighboring state.

Every home has also been designed to be flexible – with interior options pre-created for customers to choose from through a special software created by the developers. From changing wall positions, to selecting the shelving inside the cabinetry and selecting from several different finishes, the customer can completely personalize his / her home.

3D view of the entire site with
1. Green roof villas
2. Private garden – villas
3. Terrace garden at apartments
4. Terrace garden at apartments
5. Landscaped terrce
6. Wooded area
7. Green roof at club house
8. Peripheral landscape

1. View from inside into the pool and the garden
2. View of the family space and the wooden deck

Cross section of the site through apartments & villas

1. View of the living space and the terrace garden
2. View from outside into the living space
3. Living space
4. View of the family space and the glass deck

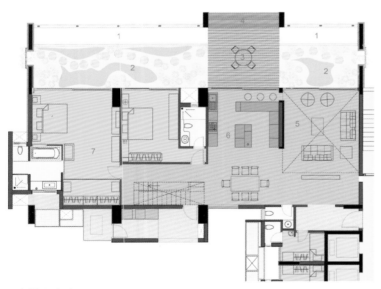

1. Water body
2. Landscape terrace
3. Wooden deck
4. Seating
5. Living
6. Kitchen & dining
7. Master bedroom

Prime Nature Residence

The project welcomes the constraints of site and programme as a framework to which molds the Shadow House into a living place filled with playful and imaginative shadow and reflection, and into architecture unique for its location and for its owner.

Completion date:
2011
Location:
Samutprakarn, Thailand
Designer:
Department of ARCHITECTURE
Photographer:
Wison Tungthunya
Area:
480 sqm (excluding parking and roof deck)

Project Description:

The owner's brief for his residence seems at first rather simple – his bedroom on ground floor, another bedroom for his mother and sister on first floor, a large interior living space, and an outdoor terrace for the mother who enjoys outdoor leisure. However, a great challenge comes with the site location. The plot is situated at a busy 3-street intersection in an up-scale residential estate that forbids the use of any kinds of fences. This constraint poses serious questions on privacy of the residents living on ground level as well as the problem of trespassing car headlights at night.

In order to cope with the sitelimitations, a conventional linear fence is broken into series of smaller vertical planes. These planes are projected onto a grid at varying distances from the house thus blocking out intruding views and simultaneously permitting ventilation into the outdoor area. The planes continue horizontally above the entire terrace creating a well-defined semi-outdoor living space.

The planes are made from two materials: metal lattice screens and sheer canvas panels which both allow partial vision from looking

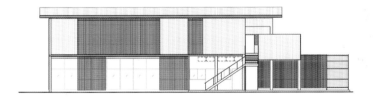

1. The building is surrounded by trees, which provides a sense of privacy
2. Wooden patio outside is enclosed by vertical panels
3. Resting chairs and tables are arranged under the grids and trees

through them. Lattice panels and swaying trees cast delicate and moving shadow patternson terrace floor, building elevations and canvas planes. A large shallow pond further adds intricacy of reflective shadow to the scene.

At night, periphery trees catch trespassing car headlights and cast their shadows on deliberately-placed canvas planes. The shadow images appearing on series of canvases fade in and out and move from one side to another depending on direction and speed of passing vehicles, reminding us of some black and white animations on movie screens.

What resulted from this is an alfresco space that is in constant flux during days and nights – a space where its qualities are defined autonomously by external forces: the wind, the sunlight, and the car lights.

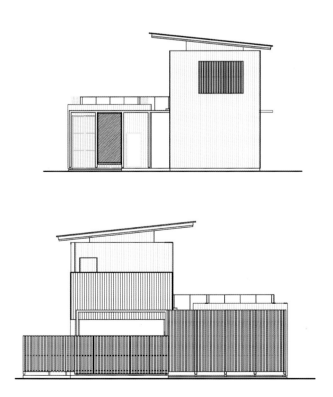

255

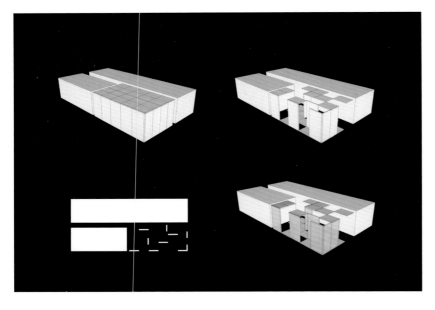

1. Semi-enclosed terrace with trees
2. Terrace and living room

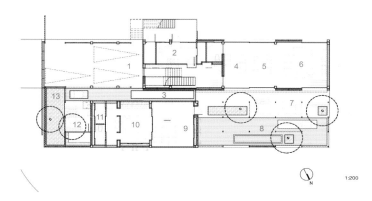

1:200

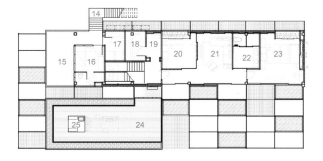

1. Parking
2. Kitchen
3. Walkway
4. Pantry
5. Dining
6. Living
7. Outdoor living
8. Pond
9. Living
10. Master bedroom
11. Master bathroom
12. Deck
13. Birdcase

14. Service stair
15. Washing area
16. Maid
17. Laundry
18. Storage
19. Buddhist altar
20. Bedroom-2
21. Living
22. Bathroom
23. Bedroom-3
24. Roof deck
25. Cdu area

a21house

Back to the a21house, an existing tree is acknowledged as the core of the house and the furniture, which is related to people activities, are arranged around that core. Therefore, people lives are occurred in an open and well ventilated space, while they still can find a comfortable place for their own activities.

Completion date:
2012
Location:
Hochiminh, Vietnam
Design firm:
a21studio
Photographer:
Hiroyuki Oki
Area:
40 sqm

Project Description:

"Every morning, the first thing that I would like to have is drawing first lines in a comfortable and joyful mind. I used to dream of an office-house for not travelling in a frequent traffic-jam and highly polluted place like Hochiminh City." The owner-designer said.

Within a limited budget, an unusual small non-square shape plot, just took ten minutes to the city central, seems to be the best choice to make the dream come true. The forty square metres polygon plot faced to a public ground, with only one and a half metre width in front, located at the end of a lane, surrounded by other neighbour houses' tall-walls, are big challenges to design an airy

office-house for four employees including a couple with a child.

Standing in this small and cramped space at the first time, instead of reluctantly thinking of green, environmentally sustainable or eco-architecture…, a wild-cage, capturing nature, in which sunlight, wind, rain-water, and trees define human activities, becomes the inspiration of a21 house.

In the concept, the designers consider the site is filled with nature. Then, when people come, they are given enough spaces to operate their activities and leave the rest freely developed as in nature. They believe that this

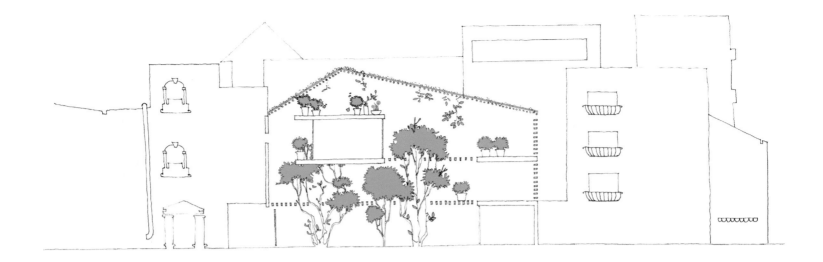

1st Floor
1. Kitchen
2. Planting location

2nd Floor
1. Office
2. Wood cutout location
3. Tree

3rd Floor
1. Bedroom
2. Void
3. stair

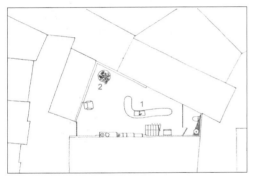
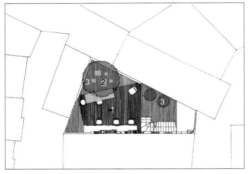
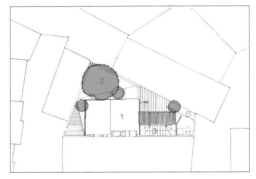

1. Exterior
2. Void
3. Bedroom to void
4. Office

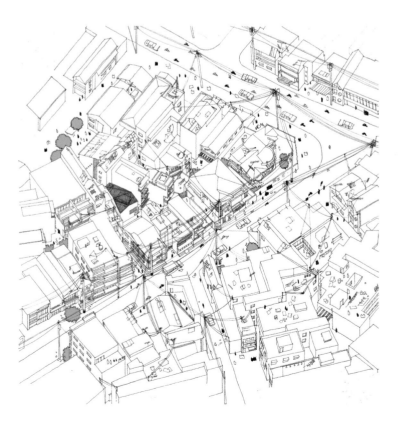

can be applied to different situations. By doing this, they would like to remind us the old good days, when nature was all around us and man feel the changing of nature and enjoyed their lives.

Lighting, intentionally directed to thread through the interstices of the floor's wooden sticks that are installed side-by-side or in different slot depended on functional space, is led from the roof to the ground floor to illuminate the narrowest corners of the house.

An open-air space with an averrhoa carambola, located at the acute angle of the house and closely connected to office area, is not only purposely "squared" the office and bedroom area, but also created an opportunity for sunlight, even water-rain and wind to naturally blow in.

"Nowadays, every morning, sitting beside the tree with a cup of coffee reflecting glisten leafs in the early morning sun-light, harmonised with soft and gentle melody, I think of the next drawings for on-progress projects." The designer said.

1. Stairs
2. Terrace down to 3rd floor
3. View from bed to toilet
4. Bedroom to void
5. Kitchen

M11 House

To integrate with nature, the architect brought the garden into home, merging it with the design. The area where the principal tree is planted almost resembles another room. The confined space it occupies means that the sound of its leaves is captured between the walls, resonating and bringing back the memories of the client's hometown.

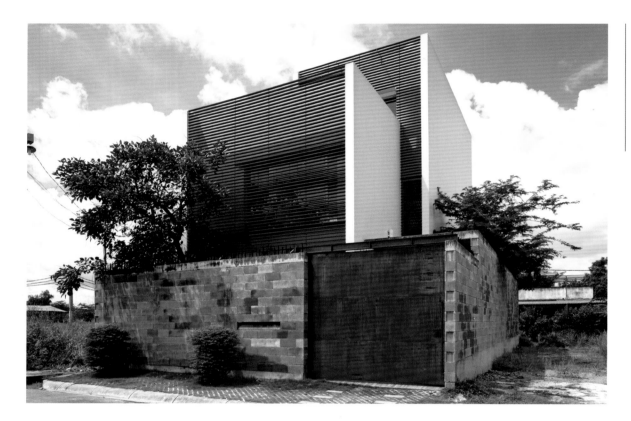

Completion date:
2008
Location:
Hochiminh city, Vietnam
Designer:
a21 studio
Photographer:
Hiroyuki Oki
Area:
150 sqm

Project Description:

M11 house is located in a suburban area in Hochiminh City. By using natural materials as wood and stone, utilising top lights as well as placing small green-courtyards inside the house, the architect wants to bring out elegant and peaceful spaces to the client who can leave all his tiring behind after a long working day to enjoy his own space in a noisy and polluted environment of a developing city.

The client admits that he was greatly influenced by the designers as they worked closely together on the project, meeting every weekend to share coffee and discuss progress. "I admired minimalism already, but Hiep (the name of designer) urged me far more strongly toward it. I also wanted to use a lot of steel. It's what was expected too because my year – the year I was born – is

a metal year. Hiep guided me away from metal however, something most Vietnamese pals would not allow". The client now concedes that the designer was right and that the wood fosters welcome warmth in the home, and besides, there are one or two concessions to his love of steel, such as Le Corbusier chair.

Wood is used extensively throughout the home, softening the concrete flooring and the colossal column that dominates at its core. Together they chose nose flute wood for its bright colour and, more practically, its anti-white ant properties.

From start to finish the project spanned three year. Over that time, the client and designer formed a tight friendship and unlikely design team, while the client's wife, who initially scepti-

cal about the plans, grew to love the house. "Now I can't pick a favourite part", she says, "If I lie down on the sofa, I feel like the sky is in the house. I also adore our bedroom and how the three outside the window is like a picture, but then I love our family room. It's all perfect."

1. Dining room looking to the garden
2. Stair to family room
3. Back garden
4. Toilet on the 2nd floor

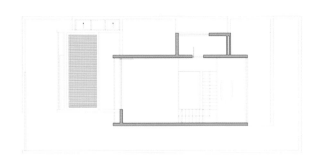

Section
1. Glass roof
2. Pond
3. Gym
4. Bathroom
5. Rock garden
6. Family room
7. Master bedroom
8. Living room
9. Dining room
10. Bedroom
11. Garden

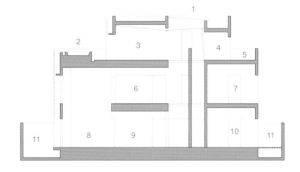

Ground Floor Plan
1. Entrance
2. Garage
3. Garden
4. Dining room
5. Living room
6. Kitchen
7. Storage
8. Bedroom
9. Toilet
10. Pond

267

Vitrea Suite

Nutritional elements are administered in the same way as with a common house plant. It is odorless and answers the need for nature, providing a daily enjoyment. The substrate is sphagnum moss, a natural plant product.

Completion date:
2011
Location:
Milan, Italy
Designer:
Alberto Apostoli
Photographer:
Luca Casonato
Area:
64 sqm

Project Description:

The concept is centred on vitreous ceramic, the recycled and recyclable material obtained from heating and fusion of recovered glass chips, which matches technical and aesthetical characteristic of glass and natural stone. It's a material of notorious expressive and technical capacities, a product that joins technology, sensuousness, aesthetic and respect for inescapable values connected to sustainability.

It has been used in indoors and outdoors of the design molded in the furniture, such as table, bed, and in some architectonical elements, as the bathrooms "bubbles" backdrop. The design was born with the intention to merge innovative materials research and sus-

tainability. Apostoli started from this product features to interpret two aspects through rational shapes, alternating blanks and full, modulated lighting and scenic attention

The living wall was provide by the Italian company Ortisgreen. The living wall (not to be confused with green wall) is a customisable composition in a vertical system – an indoor vertical garden. It is a picture with a powerful emotional impact, but with the added bonus of providing beneficial effects. Irrigation is simplified by a system that optimises the watering process.

1. The living wall is set between the bedroom and the dining room
2. The bathroom sink is also made of glass ceramic
3. Decorative lights in the small pond
4. A very modern design of dining area

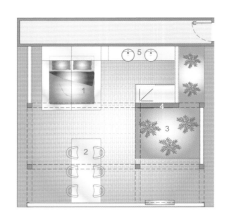

1. Bedroom
2. Dining
3. Indoor garden
4. Living wall
5. Washing area

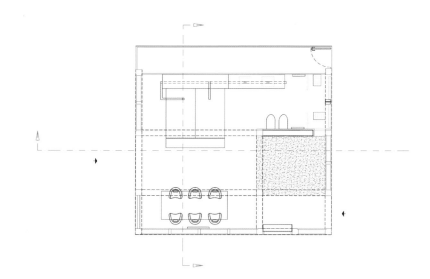

There is a structure in iron steel that substain the box in recycled alluminium. The boxes are of 50x50cm. In these boxes we put a soil where the plants lives. At the top of every box (every 50cm. high) there is a drop line to give water to the plants. The water flow is controlled by a smart valve controller.

Index